THE SMALL BUSINESS FINANCE BIBLE

3 IN 1

*The Ultimate Guide to Taxes, Bookkeeping, and Accounting
How to Minimize Taxable Income, Optimize Profit Margins,
and Prevent IRS Penalties*

Arthur P. Beaumont

© COPYRIGHT 2024 BY ARTHUR P. BEAUMONT - ALL RIGHTS RESERVED.

All rights reserved. No part of this book may be reproduced in any form without permission in writing from the author. Reviewers may quote brief passages in reviews.

While all attempts have been made to verify the information provided in this publication, neither the author nor the publisher assumes any responsibility for errors, omissions, or contrary interpretation of the subject matter herein.

The views expressed in this publication are those of the author alone and should not be taken as expert instruction or commands. The reader is responsible for his or her own actions, as well as his or her own interpretation of the material found within this publication.

Adherence to all applicable laws and regulations, including international, federal, state and local governing professional licensing, business practices, advertising, and all other aspects of doing business in the US, Canada or any other jurisdiction is the sole responsibility of the reader and consumer.

Neither the author nor the publisher assumes any responsibility or liability whatsoever on behalf of the consumer or reader of this material. Any perceived slight of any individual or organization is purely unintentional.

TABLE OF CONTENTS

INTRODUCTION   8

Overview Of the Book's Structure and What to Expect 9

SMALL BUSINESS TAXES   11

UNDERSTANDING SMALL BUSINESS TAXES   13

Small Business Tax Regulations and Filing Requirements 15
Different Types of Taxes 17
Key Terminology and Concepts in Small Business Taxation 22

MINIMIZING TAX LIABILITY   25

How to Maximize Deductions and Credits Legally 28
Leveraging Retirement Accounts and Employee Benefits 29

SPOTTING LOOPHOLES AND AVOIDING PENALTIES   32

Legal Tax Loopholes That Can Benefit Small Businesses 35
Guidelines For Avoiding IRS Penalties and Interests 38

NAVIGATING AUDITS AND INSPECTIONS   40

Preparing For and Handling IRS Audits 41
Keeping Your Business Compliant with Tax Laws 43
What To Do If You Disagree with An Audit Finding 45

PROACTIVE TAX PLANNING   48

Strategies for Year-Round Tax Planning 49
Making Estimated Tax Payments Accurately 51
Utilizing Professional Help Effectively 53

ACCOUNTING FOR SMALL BUSINESS — 56

SETTING UP YOUR ACCOUNTING SYSTEM — 58

Setting Up and Managing Your Accounting System 61
Integrating Your Accounting System with Other Business Processes 63

MANAGING CASH FLOW, BUDGETING, AND FORECASTING — 65

How To Create and Manage Budgets 67
Forecasting Future Financial Performance 69

LOANS, INVESTMENTS, AND EQUITY FINANCING — 73

The Impact of Debt and Equity on Financial Statements 76
Strategies For Financing Growth 77

UNDERSTANDING FINANCIAL STATEMENTS — 80

Balance Sheets, Income Statements, And Cash Flow Statements 81
How To Read and Interpret These Documents 82
Common Pitfalls In Financial Analysis 85

ADVANCED ACCOUNTING TECHNIQUES — 88

Internal Controls for Preventing Fraud 89
Time-Saving Automation in Accounting Practices 90
Ratio Analysis for Performance Evaluation 92

BOOKKEEPING FOR SMALL BUSINESS — 95

BASICS OF BOOKKEEPING — 97

Setting Up a Bookkeeping System: Traditional Vs. Digital Options 99

Essential Bookkeeping Tasks for Daily Operations 101

MAINTAINING ACCURATE RECORDS   104

Tips for Organizing Receipts, Invoices, and Financial Documents 107

Archival Strategies for Long-Term Record Retention 109

PAYROLL, BENEFITS, AND INDEPENDENT CONTRACTORS   111

Handling Payroll Taxes and Reporting 112

Managing Employee Benefits 114

Working With Independent Contractors 116

PERIODIC REVIEWS & RECONCILIATIONS   118

Performing Monthly Bookkeeping Checkups 119

Reconciling Bank Accounts 121

Preparing For Year-End Close-Outs 124

USING BOOKKEEPING DATA TO IMPROVE BUSINESS DECISIONS   127

Cost-Benefit Analysis for Business Investments 129

Adapting Bookkeeping Practices as Your Business Grows 131

CONCLUSION   134

APPENDICES   136

Appendix A: Glossary of Terms 136

Appendix B: Checklist for Tax Season 138

THE SMALL BUSINESS FINANCE BIBLE

INTRODUCTION

Let's make sense of the financial side of running a small business, shall we? At the heart of every thriving business lies a solid understanding of taxes, accounting, and bookkeeping. Think of these as the unsung heroes that keep your business's financial health in tip-top shape, enabling you to make smart decisions that fuel growth and stability.

Taxes can be complex, but as a small business owner, you must understand your tax obligations. This means knowing which taxes apply to your business, how to calculate them correctly, and when to pay them. Sales tax, income tax, and employment taxes are a few examples that you might need to handle. By having a good grasp of your tax responsibilities, you avoid penalties and fines associated with late or incorrect payments.

Accounting is another key area that you cannot afford to overlook. It involves recording and analyzing all of your financial transactions. This might sound daunting, but at its core, accounting gives you a clear picture of where your money is coming from and going. You might hear words like 'accounts payable' and 'accounts receivable'; simply put, these terms refer to money you owe others and money others owe you, respectively. With proper accounting practices in place, tracking your expenses becomes easier, allowing you to control costs more effectively and ensuring that you're not spending more than what's coming in.

Lastly, **bookkeeping** is the day-to-day recording of your financial transactions in an organized way. Think of it as keeping a diary for your business finances. Accurate bookkeeping helps keep track of sales, purchases, payments and receipts. While it may seem mundane compared to other aspects of running a business, it's this attention to detail that helps prevent cash flow problems.

So why are these three financial areas so important? Well for starters they help with legal compliance. Keeping accurate records ensures that you report your income and expenses correctly when it's time to file taxes. It can also protect you in case of audits; having detailed records can prove that your filings are accurate.

Understanding these financial elements also allows you to monitor the health of your business by identifying which parts are working well and which areas need improvement. You might discover

THE SMALL BUSINESS FINANCE BIBLE

through regular financial review that a particular product isn't profitable or that a specific expense category has ballooned unexpectedly.

Moreover, insights derived from accounting can empower you in negotiating better deals with suppliers or setting competitive prices for your products or services based on accurate cost analysis. And when it comes time for growth or seeking investment, detailed books will be crucial in showing potential investors or lenders that your business is financially sound and well managed.

By understanding these areas—or at least seeking out expert help—you set up your small business for financial health and long-term success. *Remember:* an investment in knowledge always pays the best interest when it comes to the financial management of your company. Make sure not to underestimate the importance of these financial foundations — they can make all the difference between just surviving and truly thriving as a small business owner.

OVERVIEW OF THE BOOK'S STRUCTURE AND WHAT TO EXPECT

If you're determined to navigate the financial complexities of a small business and optimize your monetary decisions, this comprehensive guide promises to be an invaluable companion. Anticipate an insightful layout designed to demystify the financial hurdles a small business owner typically encounters. The book is segmented into three crucial parts: *Taxes for Small Businesses, Accounting for Small Business,* and *Bookkeeping for Small Business.* Each part focuses on a core aspect of small business finance and offers practical strategies for maintaining a healthy fiscal state.

The first section of the book will take you through a deep dive into the often-intimidating world of small business taxes. You'll learn not just about different types of taxes and key terminology but also strategies on minimizing liabilities while remaining compliant with tax laws. With an emphasis on proactive approaches including year-round planning and making accurate payments, you'll gain the know-how to reduce the likelihood of penalties and master audit navigation.

Transitioning to accounting, we'll explore how to set up an accounting system that best suits your business. Topics such as cash flow management, budget creation, and forecasting will arm you with the capability to make informed predictions about your business's financial future. Additionally, we'll help you understand the nuances of managing debt versus equity financing and dissect financial statements to make them a powerful tool in your decision-making arsenal.

THE SMALL BUSINESS FINANCE BIBLE

In our final segment, bookkeeping takes center stage. You will be introduced to methods for establishing a system that meshes seamlessly with your operations, whether traditional or digital. As we cover essential tasks for sustained function, meticulous records maintenance will come into focus, equipping you with techniques for receipts management and data archiving that pave the way for long-term success.

Finally, we address advanced topics such as adapting these practices as your business grows—after all, flexibility is mandatory in bookkeeping as much as it is in business. While technical terms are commonplace when discussing finances, this guide is committed to clarity without compromising on comprehensiveness—hard-to-understand words are avoided throughout this text. *"The Small Business Finance Bible"* is more than just a guide; it's a visionary approach that promotes fiscal discipline and strategic planning while providing safeguards against detrimental IRS actions. By reading this book, you not only learn about finance but step into a role where financial foresight becomes part of your entrepreneurial skill set. Let's turn the page together towards financial clarity and control in your business endeavors.

PART 01

SMALL BUSINESS TAXES

THE SMALL BUSINESS FINANCE BIBLE

From understanding the range of taxes your business might encounter, such as income, self-employment, sales, and property taxes, this section is your map through the maze. We begin by laying out a foundation of key terminology and concepts crucial for any business owner. With this groundwork in place, we explore how you can leverage legal tax structures to enhance your financial efficiency.

We'll guide you through maximizing deductions and credits without running afoul of the law, thus keeping more money in your pocket. Saving for retirement while benefitting your business may seem like a tightrope walk; however, we demonstrate effective strategies for harmonizing these seemingly opposing goals.

In our journey together, we'll expose loopholes - not as means for evasion but as opportunities sanctioned by law that many entrepreneurs overlook. Moreover, understanding how to avoid penalties ensures that you're not paying more than what is necessary. Audits don't have to be nightmares if you're well-prepared. We'll teach you how to ready your business for potential scrutiny and maintain compliance. Should disagreements arise from audit findings, rest assured, as we also cover how to handle such disputes confidently.

Lastly, a proactive approach is crucial in tax planning. Year-round vigilance can prevent end-of-year surprises. Herein lies wisdom that could save you considerable sums when tax season arrives. This segment promises insight into balancing obedience to tax laws with the maximization of profit margins for small businesses everywhere.

CHAPTER

01

UNDERSTANDING SMALL BUSINESS TAXES

THE SMALL BUSINESS FINANCE BIBLE

When starting a business, one of the first decisions you'll make is choosing a business structure. This choice affects how much you pay in taxes, the level of your personal liability, and the ability to raise money. Let's start with the most straightforward structure – *Sole Proprietorship*. If you are a freelancer or an independent contractor, this likely applies to you. A sole proprietorship is easy to form and gives you complete control over your business. You're automatically considered to be a sole proprietor if you perform business activities but don't register as any other kind of business. Sole proprietors report their business income and expenses on their personal income tax returns (Schedule C), and earnings are subject to self-employment taxes.

Next up is *Partnership* – which includes entities like General Partnerships (GPs), Limited Partnerships (LPs), and Limited Liability Partnerships (LLPs). If your venture involves two or more individuals who want to manage and operate a business together, this could be the route for you. Under this model, each partner contributes finance and shares profits, losses, and managerial responsibilities. For tax purposes, partnerships are typically "pass-through" entities—profits pass through the business to partners who then report their share on their personal tax returns.

The *Limited Liability Company (LLC)* is like the best of both worlds, combining the simplicity of sole proprietorships and partnerships with some of the benefits of corporations. An LLC can be owned by one person (a "single-member LLC") or many people ("multi-member LLC"). From a tax perspective, an LLC itself does not pay taxes on its profits. Instead, profits are passed through to its members who then report their share of profits on their tax returns. However, an LLC can also choose to be taxed as a corporation if that's beneficial.

Speaking of corporations - they're unique entities where ownership is expressed through shares of stock. Unlike sole proprietorships or partnerships, corporations pay income tax on their profits. There are two main types: C Corporations (C Corps) and S Corporations (S Corps).

- 💵 C Corps are separate taxpayers from their owners. They're liable to corporate income tax at federal levels and possibly state levels too. After paying corporate income tax, any dividends distributed to shareholders are taxed again at the individual's own tax rate - this is often referred to as *"double taxation."*

- 💵 S Corps offers a way around double taxation. Although similar in structure to C Corps, with S Corps profits earned by the company are not taxed at the corporate level; instead, they "pass through" directly to shareholders' personal income without being subject to corporate tax rates.

THE SMALL BUSINESS FINANCE BIBLE

Now let's take a more detailed look into how these structures compare in terms of taxation:

1. **For Sole Proprietors:** Your net business income is combined with other income on your personal tax return where it's taxed at your individual rate.

2. **For Partnerships:** It requires filing an annual information return (Form 1065) for federal taxes but doesn't pay income tax itself. Instead, partners report their share of partnership income or loss on their personal tax returns.

3. **LLC Members:** Like partnerships, profit-sharing passes through members' personal income on which self-employment taxes must be paid—unless they've elected corporate taxation.

4. **C Corp Shareholders:** They confront double taxation once corporately where profits are taxed at flat rates depending on current law – usually 21% federally – then personally when dividends are distributed as mentioned earlier.

5. **S Corp Shareholders:** While avoiding double taxation can mean significant savings especially if corporate profits aren't distributed but reinvested into growing your enterprise! Each shareholder pays taxes based on their individual tax rates for their divided shares of profit—even if not all earnings were disbursed as dividends.

Understanding these nuances will inform which structure best suits your venture's financial goals while optimizing your tax commitments effectively. Always remember that while some structures may offer attractive benefits in terms of liability protection or operational ease—they might carry heavier burdens come tax season or vice versa. Therefore, gauge your businesses' financial potential against possible fiscal duties before settling on a structure.

SMALL BUSINESS TAX REGULATIONS AND FILING REQUIREMENTS

Understanding small business taxes can be a challenging affair, but it's critical to your success as an entrepreneur. Taxes aren't just about paying the government; they're about understanding how your business activities translate into obligations and opportunities. If you run a small business as a sole proprietorship, partnership, limited liability company (LLC), or corporation, either you or the entity itself will be required to file an income tax return. Even if your business hasn't made a profit or if it's inactive, you may still need to file.

THE SMALL BUSINESS FINANCE BIBLE

For sole proprietors and single-member LLCs, this is fairly simple: You report your business income and expenses on Schedule C, which is attached to your personal tax return (Form 1040). Partnerships and multi-member LLCs have a different form to tackle – Form 1065. While these entities don't pay taxes themselves, they need to file what's called an "information return" because the profits pass through to the partners or members who then report their share on their own tax returns.

Corporations are a different beast: they're taxed as separate entities under the law. Owners of corporations file their personal tax returns independently of the corporate return. Regular corporations use Form 1120 for this purpose, while S corporations use Form 1120S. An S corporation also files an information return because its income passes through to shareholders.

Alright, now when is all this due? Generally speaking, your business tax return is due by April 15th if your fiscal year aligns with the calendar year. If that date falls on a weekend or holiday, the deadline moves to the next business day. But there's an exception: if you run a corporation and have chosen a different fiscal year end, your deadline will be on the 15th day of the fourth month following the end of your fiscal year.

Don't forget about estimated taxes! This one trips up many new small business owners. If you expect to owe at least $1,000 in federal taxes for the year and you don't have an employer withholding these taxes for you (which is common for small business owners), then you're required to make quarterly estimated tax payments throughout the year using Form 1040-ES.

These payments are typically due April 15th, June 15th, September 15th, and January 15th of the following year. Just remember that if you fail to make these payments or underpay them, you might have penalties waiting for you come filing time.

Now how do you actually file? Thanks to technology, e-filing has become much more accessible and convenient for small businesses. You can electronically submit your forms through software approved by the IRS or by working with a qualified tax preparer who can do it on your behalf. Paper filing is still available too - just make sure everything's accurately completed and postmarked by the deadline.

Getting your documentation in order is crucial; save receipts, invoices, bank statements—anything that serves as proof of income or expense can help in case of an audit. It's wise not only from a legal

THE SMALL BUSINESS FINANCE BIBLE

standpoint but also helps in managing your finances better. A pivotal piece in making all this work smoothly is good bookkeeping practices: Track every financial transaction related to your business throughout the year. Don't mix personal and business banking. Clarity in finances helps manage taxes effectively—knowing what's coming in and what's going out sets you up for accurate reporting and could even lead to deductions that decrease your taxable income.

But remember! We are only scratching the surface here - there are plenty of nuances when it comes to tax regulations which could affect how much and what exactly you file. Consultation with a professional accountant or tax advisor tailored to your specific circumstances is always recommended.

DIFFERENT TYPES OF TAXES

Taxes might not be the most exciting aspect of running a small business, but they're certainly one of the most important. Whether you're knee-deep in the start-up phase or steering a well-established enterprise, a basic understanding of the various taxes that can apply to your business is crucial for staying compliant and optimizing your financial strategy. Let's walk through some common types of taxes that you, as a small business owner, might encounter along your entrepreneurial journey.

Income Tax

Income tax is the portion of your earnings that you share with the government. For small businesses, how much you pay and how you pay it depends on your business structure – whether you're a sole proprietorship, partnership, or corporation.

For sole proprietors and partnerships, the simplicity lies in pass-through taxation. Here's what that means: The business itself isn't taxed separately. Instead, the income earned by the business passes through to the individual owners' tax returns. You'll report your share of the profits and losses on a Schedule C form and attach it to your personal tax return (Form 1040). Corporations, on the other hand, face what's known as double taxation. The company pays corporate income tax on its profits first, and then when these profits are distributed to shareholders as dividends, they're taxed again on their individual returns.

You might wonder about deductions – those little nuggets of tax relief for certain business expenses that are both ordinary (common in your trade) and necessary (helpful for your business). These can range from office supplies to travel costs, and they serve as a way to reduce your taxable income. Remember, accurate bookkeeping throughout the year is key if you want to make sure you identify all possible lawful deductions.

Self-Employment Tax

As an entrepreneur without a traditional employer, you're responsible for paying not just income tax but also self-employment tax. This covers what an employer would typically contribute on your behalf to Social Security and Medicare. The self-employment tax rate might seem high at first glance—a total of 15.3%, comprised of 12.4% for Social Security up to an income ceiling that adjusts annually for inflation and 2.9% for Medicare with no income limit—but remember half of this (the 'employer' portion) is deductible when calculating your taxable income.

You calculate self-employment tax using IRS Schedule SE, which accompanies Form 1040 in your filing pack. It's based on net earnings from self-employment—after those deductions we spoke about are accounted for—so again, good recordkeeping throughout the year is critical. It's worth noting that if you earn above a certain threshold (which changes every year), there's an additional Medicare surtax. It's called an 'Additional Medicare Tax,' and yes—it's as serious as it sounds.

Payroll Tax

When you hire employees, the responsibility of handling payroll taxes comes into play. Payroll taxes are essentially taxes that an employer withholds from an employee's salary and pays on behalf of them. These funds are used to finance several government programs, including Social Security and Medicare.

For each pay period, you'll calculate the amount of payroll tax to withhold based on your employees' gross pay. This might seem daunting at first, but it's straightforward once you get the hang of it. A percentage gets allocated to Social Security and a separate percentage to Medicare. Remember, as a small business owner, you're not just withholding these taxes; you're also expected to contribute a matching amount from your own funds.

A key aspect to note is the Federal Unemployment Tax Act (FUTA), which is another component of payroll taxation. As an employer, you're responsible for paying FUTA without deducting it from your employees' wages. This tax funds unemployment benefits for workers who lose their jobs. It's due

THE SMALL BUSINESS FINANCE BIBLE

annually, so be sure to mark that on your calendar. Staying organized with payroll taxes is essential. Consider using payroll software or hiring a professional if managing this feels overwhelming – it could save you time and reduce errors in the long run.

Sales Tax

Sales tax is another crucial aspect that affects many small businesses, especially those that sell goods and services directly to consumers. Sales tax is a state-imposed tax collected by businesses at the point of sale and remitted to the government. It's worth mentioning that not all states impose sales tax (hello New Hampshire and Oregon!), but if you operate in one that does, understanding local regulations is important. Sales tax rates can vary by state, county, and city – adding layers of complexity to your role as a collector for the government.

For every transaction subject to sales tax, you must accurately calculate the charge based on the applicable rate for your location. This can sometimes be tricky when selling online or across different regions – being diligent about where your customers are located goes a long way in ensuring compliance. One tip for sales tax management is setting up separate accounts for collecting sales tax. That way, when it comes time to file and remit what you owe, the funds are already separated from your general business earnings – simplifying the process significantly.

While managing sales tax can feel like navigating a labyrinth at times due to various rates and exemptions (food items can be non-taxable in some places but taxed in others), staying informed is your best strategy here. There's no substitute for good-old research or seeking advice from a knowledgeable accountant familiar with local sales tax laws.

Property Tax

If you're picturing your place of residence right now, you're not off-base—similar principles apply. Property taxes are levied by local governments and are based on the valuation of a property (land or buildings) that your business owns. The tax rate can vary depending on the location and property type.

For instance, if you own an office building, a storefront or even just the land where your business operates, be expected to pay property tax. It's determined by assessing the value of your property and multiplying it by a tax rate set by your local government, often referred to as a mill rate. Annually or semi-annually, you're likely to receive a statement outlining what the jurisdiction assesses your property's worth alongside how much you owe.

What does this mean practically for a small business owner? It means budgeting for these taxes every year without fail. Neglecting property taxes can lead to penalties or in severe cases, a lien against your property—which simply put means legal claim against your assets to satisfy debt. Hence, staying informed about assessment notices and deadlines in your area is key.

Excise Taxes

Unlike broad-based taxes like sales tax that apply to many items across the board, excise taxes are targeted; they're paid when purchases are made on specific goods such as gasoline, tobacco, and alcohol or on certain activities like heavy truck usage on highways. Small businesses dealing in these goods or services directly may often need to handle these excise duties.

For example, if your enterprise manufactures or sells products like alcohol or tobacco products—perhaps a craft brewery or a local distillery—the price of these items generally includes excise tax costs that you will need to collect from consumers and remit back to the government. And if it's activities—in case you operate trucks for shipping goods across states—you might encounter federal highway use excise taxes based on mileage and vehicle weight.

It's vital to include excise tax rates in pricing strategies since they can materially impact the final price point for consumers. Depending on what sector your business specializes in exactly determines if these taxes are relevant and how often they must be reported — some monthly, others quarterly or annually.

Value-Added Tax (VAT)

Value-Added Tax, or VAT, is a consumption tax placed on a product whenever value is added at each stage of the supply chain, from production to the point of sale. Unlike sales tax, which is only charged on the final sale to consumers, VAT is collected incrementally by businesses throughout the production and distribution process.

So how does it affect you as a small business owner? If you're operating in a country or region where VAT is used—like many places in Europe—you'll need to add VAT to the price of the goods or services

THE SMALL BUSINESS FINANCE BIBLE

you sell. For each VAT payment you receive, you'll also be able to reclaim the VAT you've paid on your own purchases related to your business activities. This only works if your business is VAT-registered. Being registered means you'll charge VAT on your sales and claim it back on your purchases.

It's crucial for small businesses to manage VAT carefully. While dealing with VAT might feel overwhelming, tracking it systematically ensures that you're not in for a surprise when it's time to pay out. Most accounting software can handle VAT calculations for you, helping keep everything aligned with local regulations.

Estimated Tax

Switching gears now to another tax common for small business owners: the Estimated Tax. This isn't a separate type of tax but rather a method of paying the taxes that you likely already know—like income and self-employment taxes.

Estimated tax payments are used to cover not only income tax but Social Security and Medicare taxes as well—essentially encompassing self-employment tax. They're required in situations where there isn't an employer withholding these taxes from a paycheck; hence, sole proprietors, partners, and S corporation shareholders often need to pay estimated taxes.

As its name suggests, estimated taxes are based on an estimation of your earnings for the current year. Therefore, calculating how much you owe requires clear financial records and perhaps a little forecasting based on previous years' profits or losses.

Making accurate estimations is pivotal because if you underpay throughout the year—whether intentionally or accidentally—you may be subject to penalties and interest charges when it comes time to reconcile with annual tax returns. To avoid this situation, aim to pay at least 90% of what you expect to owe for the current year or 100% of last year's tax liability (the percentage may vary based on incomes; consult IRS guidelines or a local equivalent).

Remember that this isn't an exhaustive list – depending on your specific industry or location; there may be additional local taxes or sector-specific levies that apply to your business operations. Some industries may have environmental taxes or health-related excises; others might pay tourism or utility taxes.

THE SMALL BUSINESS FINANCE BIBLE

While dealing with taxes can be complex, managing them doesn't have to be overwhelming. Setting up organized accounting practices from day one will save you countless headaches when tax season rolls around. Don't hesitate either to use tax preparation software specifically designed for small businesses or consulting with a professional accountant who can provide guidance tailored to your situation. Understanding which types of taxes apply can help ensure compliance but can also lead to identifying potential advantages such as deductions and credits reserved for small businesses which can reduce overall taxable income.

KEY TERMINOLOGY AND CONCEPTS IN SMALL BUSINESS TAXATION

Understanding small business taxation is like learning a new language. It's essential to get acquainted with the fundamental terms and concepts. Doing so can help you navigate the taxes season with confidence and ensure you're taking advantage of potential tax benefits while complying with the law. Let's explore some key terminology and concepts in small business taxation.

1. **Gross Income:** This is the total income your business earns, also referred to as sales or revenue. It includes all the money received before any deductions or expenses are taken out. Imagine it as your business's total sales before any discounts.

2. **Expenses:** These are the costs you incur to run your business. They can range from office supplies and rent to utility bills and employee salaries. Certain expenses can be deducted from your gross income which brings us to our next term, net income.

3. **Net Income**: After deducting allowable expenses from your gross income, you're left with net income. This figure represents the actual earnings of your business, which the tax burden is based on.

4. **Tax Deduction:** A tax deduction reduces your taxable income, not directly reducing the amount of tax you owe but indirectly by lowering the income that's subject to tax. Common deductions could include business travel, equipment purchases, or insurance premiums.

5. **Tax Credit:** Unlike deductions, a tax credit directly reduces your tax bill dollar for dollar. If you qualify for a $1,000 tax credit and owe $4,000 in taxes, you'd only pay $3,000 after applying the credit.

THE SMALL BUSINESS FINANCE BIBLE

6. **Depreciation:** Over time, assets such as machinery or computers lose value; depreciation captures this reduction in value for accounting and tax purposes. Depreciation is a non-cash expense since no money is actually being spent year-to-year, but it can reduce taxable income as it's considered an expense.

7. **Audit:** An audit is when the IRS reviews your business's financial accounts to make sure information is reported accurately and according to tax laws. While most businesses may never face an audit, maintaining good records will help ensure that if one does occur, it goes smoothly.

8. **Employer Identification Number (EIN):** This is like a social security number for your business. It is required for businesses that have employees and allows the IRS to identify your business for taxation purposes.

9. **Payroll Taxes:** If your small business has employees, then payroll taxes are an essential concept. These are taxes withheld from employee wages (like income taxes) as well as taxes paid by the employer (like unemployment taxes), which fund social insurance programs such as Social Security and Medicare.

10. **Self-Employment Tax:** For sole proprietors and partners in a partnership, self-employment tax covers their contribution to Social Security and Medicare taxes since they don't have an employer withholding this for them from a regular paycheck.

11. **Estimated Taxes:** Small business owners typically pay estimated taxes. Since their income isn't subject to withholding like typical wage earners, they need to estimate how much they owe each quarter based on earnings.

12. **Sole Proprietorship**: The simplest structure where one person runs a business as an individual. Tax responsibilities include reporting all business income or losses on their personal income tax return using a Schedule C form.

13. **Partnership:** In this structure consisting of two or more people running a business together, partnerships report their financial results via an annual information return but do not pay direct taxes; instead, profits flow through to partners' personal returns.

14. **Corporation:** A corporation is an independent legal entity separate from its owners with two primary types - S corporation (or S corp) and C corporation (or C corp). Each has different taxation models; particularly notable is that C corps are taxed separately from their owners while S corps' profits pass through directly to shareholders' personal returns avoiding double taxation on corporate profits.

Understanding these basic terms spells out how various factors contribute towards calculating how much tax you have to pay—or how much refund you might anticipate! Remember that each small business is unique; therefore, consult with a professional accountant or tax advisor who will tailor advice specifically for your situation—the ultimate key to mastering small business taxation.

CHAPTER 02

MINIMIZING TAX LIABILITY

THE SMALL BUSINESS FINANCE BIBLE

As a small business owner, it's always wise to look for legitimate ways to lower your taxable income. After all, the less you pay in taxes, the more you can reinvest into your business or take home as profit. This not only shields more of your earnings from taxes but also could place you in a lower tax bracket, potentially yielding significant savings. Don't worry; we're not talking about getting in trouble with the taxman. Instead, we're focusing on smart, legal strategies that can help you maximize your earnings.

1. Maximize Deductions: One of the simplest methods to reduce your taxable income is by ensuring you claim all the deductions for which your business is eligible. Common deductible business expenses include:

   i. Office Expenses: Supplies, furniture, and equipment necessary for your office are deductible.
   ii. Travel Costs: If travel is essential for your business, expenses like flights, hotels, and per diems can be written off.
   iii. Marketing and Advertising: Money spent promoting your business is fully deductible, including website costs.
   iv. Education: Investments in further training or education related to your business can often be deducted.

Always consult with a tax professional to learn about the full range of deductions available to your specific business.

2. Employ a Retirement Plan: Investing in a retirement plan not only sets you up for future financial security but also can reduce your present taxable income. Making contributions to retirement plans such as an SEP-IRA, SIMPLE IRA, or a Solo 401(k) could decrease your taxable income substantially since these contributions are typically made pre-tax.

RETIREMENT PLAN	CONTRIBUTION LIMIT
SEP-IRA	Up to 25% of compensation or $61,000 (for 2023), whichever is less
SIMPLE IRA	$14,000 (under age 50) and an additional $3,000 (age 50 or older) for 2023
Solo 401(k)	$20,500 (under age 50) and an additional $6,500 (age 50 or older) for employee contributions; plus up to 25% of compensation for employer contributions

3. Defer Income: Another strategy involves deferring income so that it counts toward the next tax year's earnings. If you expect a large invoice payment near the end of the fiscal year and you believe next year's income will be lower or similar under current circumstances, delaying this income could result in paying less tax for the current year.

4. Consider Health Savings Accounts (HSAs): If you have a high-deductible health insurance plan, consider complementing it with a Health Savings Account (HSA). Contributions made to an HSA are tax-deductible, earnings grow tax-free, and distributions used for qualified medical expenses are also not taxed.

5. Charitable Contributions: Giving back can also help reduce taxable income. Contributions made by your small business to a recognized charity may be deductible. These can include cash donations as well as donations of goods or services.

6. Business Structure Optimization: Sometimes optimizing your taxable income involves examining whether your current business structure is still the most beneficial concerning taxes. For instance:

   i. *Switching from sole proprietorship to S corporation may help save on self-employment taxes.*

   ii. *For an LLC, choosing tax treatment as an S corporation over partnership taxation could offer savings if done correctly.*

It's always advisable to consult with a tax professional before making such changes to fully understand the implications.

7. Accelerate Deductible Expenses: If you anticipate upcoming purchases or investments necessary for operations or growth, making those expenses before the end of the tax year can increase your deductions and thereby lower your taxable income. However, ensure that these purchases are justifiable as strategic business decisions beyond just their impact on taxes.

8. Pay Close Attention to Inventory Management: Proper inventory management can impact how much income is considered taxable. Using accounting methods like FIFO (first-in-first-out) or LIFO (last-in-first-out), analyze which method serves better in reducing taxable income while still aligning with realistic inventory turnover.

THE SMALL BUSINESS FINANCE BIBLE

Executing strategies to reduce taxable income requires careful planning and often advice from tax professionals. Small businesses need every advantage they can get in today's competitive marketplace; effectively managing your tax burden is certainly one of them. As we have discussed various strategies – ranging from maximizing deductions and employing retirement plans to structuring companies appropriately – remember that consistent record-keeping is key in implementing these measures successfully.

HOW TO MAXIMIZE DEDUCTIONS AND CREDITS LEGALLY

As a small business owner, you're always looking for ways to keep more of your hard-earned cash in the bank where it belongs. Well, one of the smartest strategies is learning how to maximize your deductions and credits when it's time for taxes.

Deduction is an expense that you can subtract from your business's gross income, reducing the amount on which you're taxed. On the flip side, a credit is an amount that gets subtracted directly from your tax liability. Think of it as a direct discount on your tax bill. Documenting every penny might seem tedious, but it's worth its weight in gold come tax season. Track all business expenses diligently throughout the year. Bank statements, receipts, and logs should become your new best friends.

Now, have you heard of home office deductions? If you're working out of your house or apartment, you may be able to deduct a portion of your mortgage interest or rent, utilities, insurance, and repairs. Just make sure the space is used exclusively for business purposes. No kids' homework or family game nights in that nook!

Vehicle expenses can also give you significant savings. You have two choices here: deduct actual expenses like gas and repairs or go with the easier standard mileage rate method. Keep a meticulous logbook in case Uncle Sam comes knocking. Don't overlook retirement plans either! Contributions to plans like SEP IRAs or Solo 401(k)s lower your taxable income today and set up your future self for comfort.

Employee wages are another major deductible area. If you've got staff on board, remember their salaries are deductible. Just ensure they're reasonable and pay for actual work done. Next up – equipment depreciation. This is a way to write off purchases over time rather than all at once during the year you buy them. There's even a Section 179 deduction that lets you write off the full cost of qualifying equipment in one go!

THE SMALL BUSINESS FINANCE BIBLE

What about health insurance? If you're self-employed and paying for your own plan without access to an employer-sponsored one (like from a spouse's job), then those premiums are fully deductible. Advertising costs are superb deductions too; everything from business cards to online ads counts as long as they're purely for business promotion.

Education is often forgotten – but if it maintains or improves skills needed in your current business (think seminars or workshops), it's fully deductible. Never underestimate charitable contributions either! If your business donates money or goods to charity, those can be deductible donations.

And don't forget about credits! Credits like the Work Opportunity Credit for hiring certain groups or the Disabled Access Credit for making accessibility improvements are like hitting the savings jackpot!

A special note needs to be mentioned here regarding estimated taxes – pay these quarterly to avoid any underpayment penalties at year-end, which could take away from all those careful deductions and credits. Changes happen annually in tax laws – staying updated cannot be overstated. When in doubt or when things get overly complex (because sometimes they do), don't hesitate to seek professional help from an accountant who loves digging into tax codes as much as you love running your business.

LEVERAGING RETIREMENT ACCOUNTS AND EMPLOYEE BENEFITS

For many small business owners, the concept of retirement may seem like a distant priority, overshadowed by the immediate demands of managing and growing their enterprise. However, savvy entrepreneurs recognize that integrating retirement planning with their business strategy can offer substantial tax advantages. By leveraging retirement accounts and understanding employee benefits, business owners can ensure a more secure financial future for themselves and their employees while maximizing their tax efficiency.

Retirement accounts offer one of the most compelling ways for small business owners to save for the future while reducing their tax burden in the present. Accounts like 401(k)s, IRAs (Individual Retirement Accounts), SEP IRAs (Simplified Employee Pension Individual Retirement Arrangements), and Solo 401(k)s are designed with tax benefits that make them attractive savings options.

THE SMALL BUSINESS FINANCE BIBLE

A traditional 401(k) plan allows employees, including the business owner, to contribute pre-tax dollars, which can significantly lower their taxable income. In turn, this reduces the amount of taxes owed each year these contributions are made. The funds then grow tax-deferred until they are withdrawn during retirement when one's tax bracket may be lower.

SEP IRAs are particularly advantageous for self-employed individuals or small business owners with few or no employees. Contributions to a SEP IRA are tax-deductible, reducing your taxable income in a similar manner to a traditional 401(k). This type of plan also allows for larger contributions compared to traditional IRAs, thus enabling substantial tax-deferred growth potential.

A Solo 401(k) is an excellent option for sole proprietors with no employees other than a spouse. This account type allows for high contribution limits as in customary 401(k) plans but is tailored to fit the unique circumstances of an entrepreneur without staff.

For those who qualify, Roth IRAs might present an attractive alternative despite not offering immediate tax deductions on contributions like their traditional counterparts do. The advantage here lies in future benefits: qualified distributions from Roth IRAs are tax-free under current law. This means that all the growth accrued over years within a Roth IRA will not be subject to taxes upon withdrawal in retirement.

Another critical aspect often overlooked is the ability to combine health savings accounts (HSAs) with high-deductible health plans. While HSAs are primarily meant to cover medical expenses, they also serve as an additional retirement savings vehicle due to their triple-tax advantage: contributions are tax-deductible, earnings grow tax-free, and withdrawals for qualified medical expenses are not taxed.

Business owners should also pay attention to other fringe benefits that can offer tax advantages. For instance, offering flexible spending accounts (FSAs) can reduce employees' taxable income since they use pre-tax dollars to pay for eligible expenses such as child care or out-of-pocket medical costs.

Company-sponsored life insurance policies can also be a cost-effective benefit offering further tax relief since premiums paid by the company are typically deductible as a business expense and do not count as taxable income for employees receiving coverage up until certain limits. Educational assistance programs present another opportunity; when structured correctly, these programs enable employers to deduct expenses involved in funding employees' education related to their job without increasing staff's taxable income up until an IRS-specified limit annually.

It's crucial for small business owners not just to implement these strategies but also maintain vigilance over evolving tax laws that might affect retirement plans and employee benefits. Staying informed and consulting with financial advisors or accountants ensures that strategies remain compliant with regulations while optimizing potential tax advantages.

CHAPTER 03

SPOTTING LOOPHOLES AND AVOIDING PENALTIES

THE SMALL BUSINESS FINANCE BIBLE

Tax filing is an intricate process that can be fraught with mistakes, especially for small business owners who juggle myriad responsibilities. Recognizing common errors and learning how to avoid them can save time, money, and stress. One frequent mistake is *missing the filing deadline*. To avoid this, mark the tax calendar early in the year and set reminders for important dates. The Internal Revenue Service (IRS) usually requires taxes to be filed by April 15th unless it falls on a weekend or holiday; then it's the next business day. For those who need more time, filing for an extension before the deadline can prevent late-filing penalties.

Another error plaguing small businesses is *misreporting income*. All income must be reported to the IRS, including cash transactions that might not come with a formal statement. Keep meticulous records of all income throughout the year and cross-check these against any 1099s or other income statements received.

Improper deduction of expenses can lead to significant issues with tax filings. Understand what qualifies as a deductible business expense. Common allowable deductions include business supplies, home office expenses, travel costs, and employee salaries – but personal expenses are not deductible. Always verify if you're adhering to the current tax rules concerning deductions.

Small businesses must also be aware of their *obligation to pay self-employment taxes* when applicable. This type of tax covers Social Security and Medicare contributions and is often forgotten by new entrepreneurs. If you are self-employed, make sure to calculate these taxes accurately or use IRS resources available online for assistance.

Classification of employees versus independent contractors is another area prone to mistakes. Incorrectly classifying workers as independent contractors when they meet the criteria for employees can lead to significant employment tax liabilities. Review the guidelines set by the IRS to ensure correct worker classification.

THE SMALL BUSINESS FINANCE BIBLE

Here's a simple chart summarizing common errors and tips on avoiding them:

COMMON MISTAKE	HOW TO AVOID IT
Missing Filing Deadline	Mark calendar for deadlines; set reminders; file for an extension
Misreporting Income	Keep detailed records; double-check against received statements
Improper Deduction of Expenses	Learn about allowable deductions; keep personal & business separate
Not Paying Self-Employment Taxes	Calculate these taxes correctly; use IRS resources
Misclassifying Workers	Review IRS guidelines for employee vs contractor classification

Failing to keep good records throughout the year is a pervasive issue that leads to several of these errors. Implement a reliable accounting system and review your financial status regularly throughout the year—not just at tax time—to maintain accurate records. Not using professional help when needed can cost businesses more in the long run. Tax laws are complex and change frequently, so consider consulting with a tax professional or accountant who can help navigate through regulations and utilize strategies that could lower your taxable income.

Furthermore, not checking one's return for accuracy or filing with incorrect information can lead to penalties or audits from IRS. Before submitting your tax documents, review them thoroughly. Errors like wrong Social Security numbers, incorrect bank account information for direct deposit, or simple miscalculations can delay refunds or result in fines.

Many small business owners operate under multiple states or local jurisdictions which have their own set of tax rules leading to potential pitfalls like failing to file in every state where the business operates. Understand your tax responsibilities in all regions where your business has a nexus—such as physical presence, employees, or significant sales—and comply accordingly.

Overlooking carryover items such as capital losses or charitable contribution deductions that exceeded limits in previous years are also commonly overlooked. These items can often reduce taxable income in subsequent years if applied correctly.

THE SMALL BUSINESS FINANCE BIBLE

The key measures small business owners must take include staying organized with documentation; remaining informed on current tax laws affecting their business sector; leveraging professional guidance; confirming accuracy before submission; understanding state and local obligations; and utilizing carryover items judiciously. Avoiding these common missteps will secure a smoother path through tax season and safeguard against unnecessary financial burdens being imposed on your entrepreneurial venture.

LEGAL TAX LOOPHOLES THAT CAN BENEFIT SMALL BUSINESSES

Legal tax loopholes are essentially provisions within the tax code that allow individuals and businesses to reduce their taxable income legally. For small businesses, these can be particularly advantageous, as they often operate with tighter budgets and thinner profit margins than larger corporations. By taking advantage of these tax-saving opportunities, small business owners can retain more of their earnings for growth and stability.

One common loophole is the use of *retirement plans*. Small businesses can set up retirement accounts such as SEP IRAs, SIMPLE IRAs, or solo 401(k)s not only to provide retirement benefits but also to defer taxes. Contributions to these plans reduce the taxable income of the business while simultaneously preparing for the proprietor's future. For instance, a SEP IRA allows contributions of up to 25% of each employee's pay (up to a certain limit), which means substantial tax savings for a small business owner.

Another frequently overlooked tax saver for small businesses is the *home office deduction*. If you're using part of your home exclusively for business purposes, you may qualify to deduct expenses related to that portion of your home, including mortgage interest, insurance, utilities, repairs, and depreciation. It's important to note that this area must be used regularly and exclusively for business activities to qualify.

A third helpful strategy involves *depreciation*. The tax code allows businesses to write off the cost of tangible assets over time through depreciation deductions. Yet what many don't know is that Section 179 of the U.S. tax code permits businesses to deduct the entire purchase price of qualifying equipment or software within the tax year it was purchased up to a limit. This upfront deduction can significantly diminish the year's taxable income.

Moreover, small businesses can also time their income and expenses strategically. By *deferring income* into the next year and accelerating expenses into the current year, a small business can push income into a year where it expects to be in a lower tax bracket due to varying levels of projected revenue while increasing immediate deductions.

Health insurance premiums provide another break for self-employed individuals who own small businesses. These premiums are potentially deductible from their gross income. This kind of write-off acts as a boon particularly when health insurance rates continue to climb; such deductions can notably decrease net expanses.

Small businesses should also look into specific industry or local tax credits which are essentially *dollar-for-dollar reductions* in your actual tax bill as opposed to simple deductions from your taxable income. Tax credits could relate to anything from energy efficiency improvements to employment of individuals from certain target groups who have consistently faced significant barriers to employment.

Bad debts can also be converted into deductions for small business owners. If your business has provided goods or services that it hasn't been able to collect payment on, those bad debts might be deductible providing certain conditions are met including efforts have been taken to collect and there's proof that the debt is indeed uncollectible.

In addition or alternatively, depending on how they're structured legally (as LLCs, S Corporations etc.) some businesses may qualify for *"pass-through"* taxation wherein profits are taxed at individual rather than corporate rates which may constitute savings especially with recent changes in legislation affecting pass-through entities under certain conditions. Lastly, investment in so-called opportunity zones can offer significant advantages – deferring capital gains taxes on any prior investments' earnings if they're reinvested in qualified funds connected with these designated areas aimed at economic upliftment.

It's essential for small business owners not just knowing about these "loopholes" but ensuring compliance with all regulations when using them because improper usage could lead back-fires such as audits or penalties. Developing a relationship with a knowledgeable accountant or taking time thoroughly researching IRS documents is advisable here – as staying informed ensures smart decisions around taxes now help fortify your venture's financial health down-line without crossing any legal red-tapes.

To illustrate the benefits of these tax loopholes, consider the case of Jane, a freelance graphic designer who operates out of her two-bedroom apartment in a bustling city. Her business is registered as a sole proprietorship, and she's always on the lookout for ways to optimize her expenses. Jane stumbled upon the concept of the home office deduction one tax season. Though she initially doubted the difference it could make, upon further research and consulting with her tax professional, she understood that it could significantly impact her taxable income.

To comply with the IRS requirements, Jane began using one bedroom exclusively as her workspace. She carefully documented her expenses, tracking mortgage interest, property taxes, utilities, home insurance, and office supplies rigorously throughout the year. Since Jane's home office occupied 15% of her apartment's total square footage, she was able to apply that percentage to her relevant home expenses for tax deductions.

During that same year, Jane decided to upgrade her graphic design workstation and software to enhance productivity and serve her clients better. She learned about Section 179 and tapped into its benefits. By purchasing all of her equipment in one go during the final quarter of the year, including a high-end computer, dual monitors, and specialized graphic design software, Jane could deduct the entire purchase price from her gross income. This deduction considerably lowered what would've been her taxable profit for the year.

Thanks to timing these actions appropriately with the advice of her accountant – capturing deductions in a higher-income year while deferring some client billings to the new year – she was able to maximize her tax benefits while remaining compliant with regulations. Couple these practices with assigning money towards a SEP IRA fund for retirement planning – which she hadn't previously considered being self-employed – presented another layer of tax efficiency. She managed a 20% contribution margin from her net earnings which further lowered her taxable income bracket yet set her on course for future financial security.

Jane's story is not only a lesson in leveraging legal tax loopholes but also an inspiring scenario displaying how these provisions can aid an individual small business owner when appropriately and judiciously utilized. It highlights the importance of keeping abreast with tax law changes and demonstrates through real-world application how strategic tax planning contributes positively to an entrepreneur's financial journey without overstepping legal boundaries.

THE SMALL BUSINESS FINANCE BIBLE

GUIDELINES FOR AVOIDING IRS PENALTIES AND INTERESTS

Staying on the good side of the Internal Revenue Service (IRS) is crucial for small business owners. It's about keeping your finances in check and avoiding the unpleasant experiences of dealing with penalties and interest charges that can arise from tax mistakes. Here are some guidelines to follow:

1. Understand Deadlines: Timeliness is your first defense against IRS penalties. Here are steps to keep you on schedule:

   i. *Identify Key Dates:* The IRS has several deadlines for different types of payments and filings. Pinpoint each relevant deadline, like estimated tax payment deadlines, the annual tax return date, and deadlines for payroll taxes if you have employees.

   ii. *Set Reminders:* Use digital calendars or an organizing app to set reminders well before each due date, giving you ample time to prepare.

   iii. *Schedule Payments Early:* Always aim to schedule payments a few days before they're due to account for unexpected delays.

2. Maintain Accurate Records: The accuracy of your financial records significantly influences your tax reporting:

   i. *Keep Detailed Records:* Log every financial transaction related to your business accurately. This includes income, expenses, deductions, and credits.

   ii. *Separate Personal and Business Expenses:* Mixing these can create confusion and may lead to incorrect tax filings.

   iii. *Get Organized:* Regularly update your bookkeeping and store receipts as they will provide the necessary proof if the IRS questions a deduction.

3. Understand Your Tax Obligations: Knowledge is power when dealing with taxes:

   i. *Know Which Taxes You Owe:* Understand the various types of taxes that apply to your business, such as income tax, self-employment tax, employment taxes for employees (if applicable), excise taxes (for specific businesses), and others.

   ii. *Learn About Tax Changes:* Stay informed about changes in tax laws each year that may affect your business.

4. Make Accurate Estimated Tax Payments: If you're required to make estimated tax payments throughout the year (applies typically when you expect to owe $1,000 or more when your return is filed):

   i. *Calculate Estimated Payments Correctly: Use the IRS Form 1040-ES to estimate the amount you should pay.*

   ii. *Pay on Time: Make these payments by their respective deadlines through electronic funds transfer, credit card, check, or money order using the Electronic Federal Tax Payment System (EFTPS).*

5. Use the Correct Forms: Mistakes on forms can lead to penalties:

   i. *Choose Correct Forms: Ensure you're using the correct forms required for your type of business when filing taxes.*

   ii. *Double Check Entries: Before submitting any form or report, double-check all entries for accuracy.*

6. Seek Professional Help When Needed: Tax professionals can be an invaluable resource:

   i. *Consult with a Tax Advisor: If you're unsure about any aspect of your taxes or want assurance you're handling them correctly, do not hesitate to seek advice from a certified public accountant or a tax advisor familiar with small businesses.*

   ii. *Consider Professional Filing Services: A professional can help prepare and file your taxes, potentially spotting deductions or credits you might have overlooked.*

By following these guidelines faithfully and adopting proactive strategies in managing your taxes, you'll be better equipped to avoid unnecessary complications with the IRS—leaving you free to focus on growing your small business rather than fretting over fiscal fines.

CHAPTER

04

NAVIGATING AUDITS AND INSPECTIONS

THE SMALL BUSINESS FINANCE BIBLE

PREPARING FOR AND HANDLING IRS AUDITS

Confronting an IRS audit can be a challenging time for any small business owner. However, with the right preparation and understanding, you can navigate through the process with confidence. It is vital to maintain clear and detailed records of all business transactions. Keep a well-organized filing system, whether it's physical folders or digital spreadsheets, with invoices, receipts, bank statements, and tax documents that are readily accessible. Make it a routine to update these files regularly to avoid last-minute hassles.

Understanding the types of audits is also important. The IRS may conduct a mail audit, office interview audit, or field audit. The mail audit is the simplest; you'll need to send in documentation to clear up specific issues. For an office or field audit, it's more in-depth and either held at an IRS office or at your place of business.

Now, if you receive a notification from the IRS indicating that you will be audited (usually through mail), do not ignore it. Promptly read through the details so you understand why you're being audited and what documents are needed. Consulting with a tax professional can be invaluable at this stage to get expert advice on how to proceed. Once you've got your documentation ready and reviewed by a professional if possible, organize them according to the year or category as requested by the IRS notice. It will save time during the actual audit if everything is systematically arranged.

When dealing with the actual audit process:

1. Make sure only to provide what is asked for by the auditor; do not offer more information than necessary as it could open up other issues.
2. Answer questions honestly but succinctly.
3. If you're unsure about any question asked during the audit, it's okay to let them know that you'll need to verify information before answering.
4. Be courteous but firm; remember that you have rights during an audit and one of them includes not being forced into a quick answer without adequate consideration.

Taking care of potential discrepancies before they occur is another way to handle audits efficiently. For instance:

1. **Double-check your deductions:** Make sure that what you claim fits IRS guidelines.

THE SMALL BUSINESS FINANCE BIBLE

2. **Report all income:** Don't overlook any income no matter how small it might seem.
3. **Reconcile returns filed with daily bookkeeping records throughout the year:** This helps catch mistakes early.

In case there are findings post-audit that require rectification:

1. Ask for clarification if there's anything in their report you don't understand.
2. If errors are minimal and lead to additional taxes owed, it may be wise just to pay them promptly.
3. For larger discrepancies leading to significant tax liabilities, consult your tax professional on possible resolutions which may include setting up payment plans or contesting findings via appeals.

Remember that penalties for inaccuracies depend on whether mistakes were made inadvertently or deliberately. Willful evasion has severe consequences while honest errors might just lead to interest charges on unpaid taxes.

Lastly, learn from the audit experience:

- 💵 Work with your tax advisor on any recommended changes in keeping financial records or reporting income and expenses.
- 💵 Conduct internal reviews periodically especially after changes in tax laws.

Note that audits can happen randomly but often occur because something triggered a red flag in your tax return such as discrepancies between reported figures and average norms for similar businesses.

Preparation for an IRS audit does not start when you receive notification; rather good business practices carried out consistently form your best preparation game plan. By keeping accurate records, being aware of common triggers for audits, enlisting professional help when necessary, and handling all dealings with the IRS professionally and calmly, your business will not only survive an audit but emerge having reinforced good financial habits.

THE SMALL BUSINESS FINANCE BIBLE

KEEPING YOUR BUSINESS COMPLIANT WITH TAX LAWS

Understanding and adhering to tax laws are crucial for any small business owner. To ensure that your business remains compliant and ready for any audits or inspections, there are several important steps you can take.

Know your obligations. Tax laws vary depending on your location, the type of business you run, and whether you have employees. Generally, businesses must pay income tax on their earnings and collect sales tax from customers if applicable. If you have employees, you're also responsible for withholding a portion of their earnings for taxes and contributing to social security or other government programs.

Maintain meticulous records. Keeping detailed records not only helps in preparing accurate tax returns but also serves as evidence of your financial transactions should an audit occur. Ensure all receipts, invoices, bank statements, payroll records, and other relevant documents are systematically stored either physically or electronically.

Catalog business expenses properly. Organize your expenses into categories such as office supplies, travel, and entertainment. Some expenses are fully deductible while others only partly. Separating personal and business costs is crucial – a common mistake is mixing the two.

Leverage technology like accounting software to track income and expenses accurately throughout the year. This aids in real-time financial monitoring, which helps detect errors early on and keeps your books audit-ready at any time.

Estimated tax payments are required if you expect to owe a certain amount in taxes for the year. Paying estimated taxes helps avoid penalties at year-end. Usage of tax calendars or reminders can ensure that no deadlines are missed.

Get familiar with tax deductions and credits relevant to small businesses which can significantly reduce taxable income. Additionally, understanding how depreciation works with capital expenses can provide significant savings over time.

Consider professional help if needed. Tax professionals can offer valuable advice tailored to your business needs, especially when dealing with more complex issues like multi-state tax compliance or international tax laws.

THE SMALL BUSINESS FINANCE BIBLE

Know what triggers an audit. While sometimes random, audits can also result from consistent losses reported, excessive write-offs compared to similar businesses or late filings, among other red flags.

If subject to an inspection or audit, stay calm and cooperative. Have all requested documents organized and ready to present; never obstruct the process as it could lead to further inquiry or suspicion.

Create a checklist of compliance checkpoints throughout the year: It could be monthly review of bookkeeping entries or quarterly tax filings—remain proactive rather than reactive when it comes to compliance.

SMALL BUSINESS COMPLIANCE CHECKLIST

COMPLIANCE ACTIVITY	DESCRIPTION	FREQUENCY	DOCUMENTED (YES/NO)
Recordkeeping	Track all financial transactions	Daily	Yes
Separate Business Accounts	Keep personal and business finances separate	As transactions occur	Yes
Expense Categorization	Organize expenses into proper categories	Weekly/Monthly	Yes
Estimated Tax Payments	Pre-pay expected taxes	Quarterly	Yes
Deductions & Credits Review	Identify possible deductions/credits before tax filing	Annually	
Professional Consultation	Seek experts' advice on complex matters (accountants/lawyers)	As needed	

Lastly, keep abreast of changes in tax law that may affect your business; this includes new deductions or changes in reporting requirements by staying informed either through reading reputable sources or attending seminars provided by tax authorities or professional bodies within your industry.

THE SMALL BUSINESS FINANCE BIBLE

WHAT TO DO IF YOU DISAGREE WITH AN AUDIT FINDING

Understanding the nuances of audit findings is critical for any small business owner. If you find yourself disagreeing with an auditor's result, it's essential to approach the situation calmly and strategically. It's vital to know that auditors have a responsibility to report their findings objectively and based on evidence. Their role is not adversarial. If their finding is unfavorable, it doesn't necessarily mean they are correct, but it does entail that they have identified what they believe to be a discrepancy or issue that needs addressing.

When you disagree with an audit finding, commence by thoroughly reviewing the auditor's report. Understand exactly why they arrived at their conclusion. The report should detail the specific areas of non-compliance or concern, as well as the evidence the auditor used for their decision-making. Read through these details carefully; understanding the auditor's perspective is essential before crafting your response.

After reviewing the report, gather your documentation and records relevant to the disputed finding. Your records should be complete and organized, making it easy to pinpoint where you might believe the auditor has made an error. You'll need to present clear evidence that counters the auditor's claim if you hope to dispute their findings successfully.

Next, draft a written response to the audit finding. Your response should be professional and precise; this is not a personal attack but rather a business communication where clarity is vital. Begin by stating your respect for the audit process and your commitment to financial integrity and compliance. Outline your disagreement clearly, referring specifically to parts of the audit report which you believe are incorrect or have been misinterpreted. Provide your evidence in an organized manner so that it directly relates to each point of contention you're disputing.

It may be worth discussing your draft with someone familiar with audits but who also understands your business - perhaps an accountant or a financial advisor who can provide insight into whether your disagreement has merit from an auditing standpoint. Once satisfied with your draft, submit your written response to the auditors within their specified deadline timeframe. It's essential not only that you respond but that you do so promptly - demonstrating professionalism and a proactive approach in resolving issues.

If possible, request a meeting with the auditors after they have reviewed your written response. A face-to-face conversation can sometimes clear up misunderstandings more quickly than written communications. Be sure to enter this meeting well-prepared, with all relevant documents on hand for reference. Remember that auditors are bound by standards and must maintain independence; however, sensible auditors are open to discussion and willing to consider additional information that could impact their findings.

If after discussing things both parties still cannot agree upon corrected conclusions, consider what pathways are available for further disputes. This may involve arbitration or speaking with higher levels in the auditing firm about your concerns. Be aware that this route can be lengthy and potentially costly. It would help if you weighed up whether such an endeavor is worth its potential benefits.

Sometimes accepting an auditor's finding – even if disagreed upon – could be more cost-effective than pursuing further dispute processes when considering time and resources involved – especially in cases where rectifying issues could improve business practices moving forward.

Whether in agreement or dissent with audit results, use this as a learning opportunity. Understanding what led to disputed findings can form part of risk management planning for future protocols in your business operations. Taking steps towards improvement can prevent similar issues from arising again down the line and demonstrates good faith towards regulatory compliance among those observing your business affairs – which can ultimately be beneficial for your company's reputation.

Now, let's examine a real-life example that brings the principles to life:

Jim owns a small electronics repair shop, *'QuickFix Electronics,'* which has been operational for six years. The business has seen steady growth, but with that growth has come increased scrutiny from regulatory authorities. Last year, the business underwent a routine audit, and Jim was surprised to find that the auditors had flagged several transactions as non-compliant with tax regulations.

The auditors' report indicated that QuickFix Electronics claimed expenditures on equipment that were not eligible for tax deductions. According to the report, these items did not meet the criteria set by tax authorities for necessary business expenses.

THE SMALL BUSINESS FINANCE BIBLE

Jim, confident in his tax compliance practices, disagreed with these findings. He began by carefully reviewing the auditor's report and found that the audit had failed to acknowledge that the items in question were actually part of a newer category of advanced diagnostic tools essential for modern electronics repair – an error that stemmed from an outdated understanding of what constituted necessary equipment in his field.

Armed with his knowledge and documentation, Jim compiled a comprehensive written response. He collected invoices, operational manuals, and industry reports that illustrated the necessity of these advanced tools for a contemporary electronics repair shop. He meticulously matched each piece of evidence to contradict the auditors' claim.

In his response to the auditors, Jim remained respectful and factual. He acknowledged their efforts but pointed out where their assessment had not kept pace with industry standards. With clarity and precision, he detailed the nature of each tool, its use in daily operations, and industry articles supporting their necessity—all while avoiding technical jargon. After submitting his argument and supporting documents within the deadline specified by the auditing firm, Jim also requested an in-person meeting to discuss his points further.

During this meeting, armed with his clear documentation and evidential support, Jim was able to walk through each concern with the auditors. After demonstrating how each tool was indeed integral to current electronics repair work and providing new perspectives on how industry practices have evolved, he found common ground with the auditors. They acknowledged their lack of familiarity with recent technological advances in his niche sector. As a result of this process—although taxing in time and resources—Jim's initial findings were amended in QuickFix's favor. The equipment expenditures were recognized as compliant deductible expenses.

Beyond resolving this specific audit finding disagreement effectively without resorting to expensive dispute processes or arbitration; Jim took away valuable lessons from this experience. He recognized gaps in how external entities might perceive industry-specific operations within his business. This insight prompted him to adopt a proactive approach towards educating others about his evolving field—for instance by including summaries about industry changes with future financial disclosures. Ultimately, taking steps like these could prevent similar misunderstandings and ease future audits — thereby safeguarding QuickFix Electronics' reputation as a professional and proactive business committed to compliance.

CHAPTER

05

PROACTIVE TAX PLANNING

THE SMALL BUSINESS FINANCE BIBLE

STRATEGIES FOR YEAR-ROUND TAX PLANNING

Tax planning shouldn't be relegated to a once-a-year event, but rather approached as a year-round activity. This consistent attention can result in significant savings and prevent last-minute scrambling. Let's delve into strategies that can help streamline tax planning throughout the year.

1. Education on Tax Changes: Staying informed about the latest tax laws can significantly impact your business decisions and tax outcomes. Changes in tax laws may introduce new deductions or credits that could benefit your business. Set aside time each month to read up on current tax news or meet with your tax advisor to stay updated.

2. Expense Tracking: Effective expense tracking is vital for small businesses. Implement a system where you log expenses as they occur, ensuring nothing slips through the cracks. Proper documentation is the key to maximizing deductions and making tax season less burdensome.

MONTHLY EXPENSE TRACKING SCHEDULE	
MONTH	**TASK**
January	Review last year's expenses; categorize new expenses.
February	Validate expense tracking system; rectify errors.
March	Prepare for possible quarterly tax payment; assess expenses and revenues.
April	File taxes; start fresh expense log for new fiscal year.
May	Update budget forecasts based on current financial trends.
June	Conduct mid-year financial review; adjust expense tracking if necessary.
July	Prepare documentation for next quarterly tax payment.
August	Review categorized expenses for optimization opportunities.
September	Third quarter check-in; ensure expense tracking aligns with current operations.
October	Initiate end-of-year tax planning discussions with advisor; forecast year-end purchases/expenses.
November	Consider deferring income if beneficial for tax purposes; finalize year-end strategies.
December	Implement final tax moves; organize financial documents for easy access in the new year.

THE SMALL BUSINESS FINANCE BIBLE

3. Maximizing Deductions: A common strategy is to track all potential deductions throughout the year, such as travel expenses, home office expenditures, or vehicle usage for business purposes. Maximizing legitimate deductions can significantly reduce taxable income.

4. Deferring Income: If possible, it may be advantageous to postpone invoicing or defer income until after the new year, reducing taxable income in the current year if you anticipate being in a lower tax bracket in the following year.

5. Retirement Planning: Contributing to a retirement plan not only helps secure your future but can also provide current tax benefits. Consider making contributions to Simplified Employee Pension (SEP) plans, 401(k)s, or similar vehicles designed for small business owners and self-employed individuals.

6. Tax Credits: Don't overlook various available tax credits, which directly reduce your amount of taxes owed rather than just decreasing taxable income like deductions do. Research credits such as those for hiring certain employees, using green energy, or providing access to disabled persons.

7. Consistent Review: Schedule quarterly reviews of your financials with your advisors to make adjustments proactively instead of reactively responding at year-end.

8. Estimated Taxes: Small business owners often need to pay estimated taxes quarterly instead of yearly to avoid underpayment penalties. Keep accurate records of income and expenses every month so that you can calculate these payments more precisely.

QUARTERLY ESTIMATED TAX PAYMENT SCHEDULE		
QUARTER	PERIOD COVERED	PAYMENT DUE DATE
First	January 1 - March 31	April 15
Second	April 1 - May 31	June 15
Third	June 1 - August 31	September 15
Fourth	September 1 - December 31	January 15 (next year)

THE SMALL BUSINESS FINANCE BIBLE

9. Debt Management: Strategically manage debt so that it can work in favor of your business while considering tax implications of interest payments and financing options.

10. Communication with Tax Professionals: It's crucial to regularly communicate with your accountant or tax advisor to discuss changes in the business or any new legislation that might affect your strategy.

By applying these strategies and establishing a disciplined approach to financial management throughout the year, you're setting up your small business not just for successful navigation through tax season but also toward overall financial health and growth.

MAKING ESTIMATED TAX PAYMENTS ACCURATELY

Running a small business has its set of challenges, and one of the most important as well as complex aspects for many owners is managing financial obligations to the government, specifically in terms of taxes. Unlike individuals who are employees and have taxes automatically withheld from their paychecks, as a small business owner, you will often need to make estimated tax payments throughout the year.

Estimated tax payments are payments are periodic prepayments on what you estimate you will owe in taxes for income not subject to withholding. This can include earnings from self-employment, interest, dividends, alimony, rent, gains from the sale of assets, prizes, and awards. If you expect to owe at least $1,000 in federal tax for your business activities after subtracting your withholding and credits, then you probably need to make estimated tax payments.

Now let's talk about how to do it accurately:

STEP 1. CALCULATE YOUR ESTIMATED TAX:

Accuracy starts with good record-keeping. Keep a detailed accounting of all your income and expenses throughout the year. Being organized helps you estimate more precisely what you'll owe. To calculate your estimated tax, you'll need to figure out your expected adjusted gross income (AGI), taxable income, taxes, deductions, and credits for the year. Use the worksheet in Form 1040-ES from the IRS to calculate your estimated tax. You'll start by estimating your expected AGI and then apply your deductions — both standard or itemized — to determine your estimated taxable income.

THE SMALL BUSINESS FINANCE BIBLE

STEP 2. UNDERSTAND YOUR TAX RATES:

Once you have an idea of your estimated taxable income, apply the applicable tax rates to calculate how much you will likely owe at year-end. The United States has a progressive tax system where the rates increase as income increases. Hence, knowing which tax bracket your earnings fall into is key to making an accurate estimation.

STEP 3. CONSIDER PREVIOUS YEAR'S TAX:

A safe way to avoid underpayment penalties is by paying at least 100% (or 110% for higher-income individuals) of your previous year's tax liability in estimated payments if your current year's earnings are unpredictable. If this method still results in underpayment penalties because of increased earnings this year compared to last year's and it was impossible for you to anticipate accurately by using prior data alone then further adjustments may be required during subsequent periods within the year.

STEP 4. MAKING PAYMENTS ON TIME:

The IRS requires that you make quarterly estimated tax payments throughout the fiscal year. Typically, these deadlines fall in April, June, September of the current year, and January of the next. If these dates fall on weekends or holidays they're due on the next business day. Not adhering to these deadlines can result in interest or penalties.

STEP 5. ADJUST ESTIMATES AS NEEDED:

As a small business owner your income might be variable so it is crucial to revisit your estimates throughout the year and make adjustments accordingly during each payment period if needed. It's important when making adjustments not just look at earnings but also consider unexpected expenses that might affect your net income. Making adjustments can help decrease penalties for underpayment and avoid overpaying which could restrict cash flow unnecessarily.

One efficient strategy to keep track of these payments is through bookkeeping software that can keep running tallies of your earnings and apply current tax rates to estimate what you owe each quarter. Regularly evaluate whether upcoming payments need adjusting; if your business picks up more rapidly than expected or encounter unexpected expenses there'll be a direct effect on your estimated tax liability.

Always remember though fluctuating cash flow between quarters is common among small businesses so consult with a tax professional if changes are substantial enough. A valuable tip is setting aside money for taxes in a separate bank account. This ensures funds are available when it's time to make a payment without affecting day-to-day business operations. Keeping good records is paramount for reasons beyond knowing how much to pay; they can be instrumental during audits or when there are questions about a return.

UTILIZING PROFESSIONAL HELP EFFECTIVELY

While many small business owners are experts in their fields, they might not have the specialized knowledge needed to navigate the complex world of taxes effectively. This is where professional help can make a significant difference, transforming a potentially stressful experience into a strategic advantage.

The first step in utilizing professional tax help effectively is finding the right advisor. Not all professionals are created equal; it's essential to choose someone with experience in small business taxation. Look for certified public accountants (CPAs) or tax attorneys who have an established track record of working with businesses similar in size and industry to your own. Personal recommendations from fellow business owners or industry associations can be invaluable here.

Once you have found someone you trust, establish clear communication. Your tax advisor should understand your business goals and financial situation. They should be approachable and capable of explaining complex tax concepts in straightforward terms that you can understand without industry jargon. Remember, their ability to advise isn't just about crunching numbers; it's about making those numbers make sense to you so that you can make informed decisions.

Working with a tax professional doesn't mean handing over the reins entirely; think of it as a partnership. Be proactive in engaging with your advisor throughout the year, not just at tax time. By

THE SMALL BUSINESS FINANCE BIBLE

doing this, you position yourself to take advantage of planning opportunities that could minimize your liabilities well before deadlines loom.

One of the many benefits of engaging a tax professional is their ability to keep up with changes in tax law that could affect your business. Tax codes are notoriously complicated and subject to frequent change, so having an expert who stays abreast of these changes can save you from costly mistakes rooted in outdated information.

Incorporating technology into this partnership amplifies its benefits. There is a plethora of financial software available that can facilitate seamless sharing of financial data with your tax advisor. Armed with up-to-date, comprehensive financial reports, they can provide more effective strategies tailored for your business's specific needs.

Your advisor can also help identify deductions and credits that you might overlook on your own. Small businesses often qualify for various deductions that might seem obscure or dauntingly complex at first glance. A knowledgeable professional will help ensure you maximize these opportunities while remaining compliant with regulations.

While taking full advantage of deductions is essential, effective proactive tax planning also involves considering future business scenarios and how they may impact your taxes. This could include expansions, investments in new equipment, hiring additional employees, or other moves that could have significant tax implications. A good advisor will help you anticipate the consequences these activities might have on your taxes and guide you towards decisions that align with efficient tax strategy.

Additionally, exploring different business structures under the guidance of your advisor can lead to substantial savings. Your current structure may have been ideal during the early stages of your business but reevaluating as your business grows or changes is important. An S corporation might offer more favorable tax rates compared to a C corporation for some businesses, for example—consulting with an expert will clarify whether restructuring could be beneficial for you.

A future-oriented approach is crucial for proactive planning—meaning considering not only next year's taxes but further ahead as well. This long-term vision includes succession planning and understanding how today's choices influence future transitions or sales of the business.

THE SMALL BUSINESS FINANCE BIBLE

Tax planning should also consider personal income and how it intersects with your enterprise; these are not always separate entities when it comes to taxation—especially for sole proprietors or partners. A sound approach employs tactics such as deferring income or strategically timing large purchases to optimize individual and business financial outcomes.

PART II

ACCOUNTING FOR SMALL BUSINESS

THE SMALL BUSINESS FINANCE BIBLE

Accounting is a language of its own that speaks volumes about the health and trajectory of your business. Part II of "The Small Business Finance Bible [3-in-1]" focuses on making accounting principles accessible and useful to small business owners. We start by guiding you through setting up an accounting system that integrates seamlessly with your daily operations—a system that will serve as the backbone of financial management within your enterprise.

Understanding cash flow is synonymous with knowing the lifeblood of your company; thus we provide practical knowledge on budget creation and management—skills fundamental to keeping your business afloat and thriving long-term. Forecasting future finances will no longer seem like peering into a crystal ball but rather making informed predictions based on solid data.

Securing loans or investments? We demystify their impact on your financial statements and offer insight into debt versus equity financing strategies that enable growth without sacrificing financial stability. Deciphering financial statements such as balance sheets and income statements is made simple here—improving your ability to make decisions based on their tales of numbers. We also explore common analytical pitfalls so that you can sidestep them expertly.

Our final offering in this section relates to advanced accounting techniques—think internal controls against fraud and time-saving automation. This knowledge serves as tools not merely for managing more effectively but also as instruments aiding strategic decision-making for better performance outcomes.

CHAPTER 06

SETTING UP YOUR ACCOUNTING SYSTEM

THE SMALL BUSINESS FINANCE BIBLE

The first step in choosing accounting software is to understand your specific business needs. *Are you a sole proprietor, or do you have employees? What is the volume of your transactions? Do you require payroll management?* Answering these questions will help you narrow down the features you need.

Once you've identified your requirements, it's time to consider what features are essential for your operations. Here are some core features to look for:

1. **User-Friendly Interface:** The software should be easy to navigate, even for those without in-depth accounting knowledge.
2. **Expense Tracking:** The ability to effortlessly monitor and categorize company spending.
3. **Invoicing:** Facilities to create, send, and manage invoices directly from the software.
4. **Tax Preparation:** Features that assist with tax-related tasks can save a great deal of time and reduce errors.
5. **Integration:** The ability to integrate with other systems like inventory management, CRM, or e-commerce platforms.

Cost is an important factor when selecting accounting software. Some software offers a flat rate while others might charge monthly or annually. Be mindful of potential add-on expenses such as setup fees, support costs, or charges for additional users.

It's crucial to choose software that can grow with your business. Project where your business will be in the next few years and select a platform that can accommodate that growth without needing to migrate your entire financial history onto a new system.

Once you've made a list of potential options based on features and cost, it's wise to review user feedback online and take advantage of free trials offered by most software companies. This will give you a firsthand experience before committing.

Since this software handles sensitive financial data, security should never be compromised. Look out for features like encryption, multi-factor authentication, and regular backups when making your decision.

THE SMALL BUSINESS FINANCE BIBLE

After thorough research and testing, compare your notes against the needs of your business, considering both present requirements and future aspirations. An informed decision now can save countless hours and resources in the long run.

Below is a comparison chart highlighting some key considerations when choosing accounting software:

FEATURE	SOFTWARE A	SOFTWARE B	SOFTWARE C
User-Friendly	✔	✔	✘
Expense Tracking	✔	✘	✔
Invoicing	✔	✔	✔
Tax Preparation	✘	✔	✔
Integration	High	Moderate	Low
Scalability	Up to 100 Users	Up to 30 Users	Unlimited
Cost	$$	$	$$$
Free Trial Available	Yes (30 days)	Yes (14 days)	No
Security Features	High	Moderate	High

Note: The symbols (✔/✘) indicate whether a particular feature is included (✔) or not included (✘). The cost is indicated by $ signs where more signs suggest higher pricing.

Selecting a suitable accounting software requires careful consideration but doesn't have to be an overwhelming task. Balancing functionality with ease of use, cost, scalability, and security should point you toward the ideal choice for your small business's financial management needs. With thoughtful research followed by hands-on testing during trial periods, you'll find technology that not only keeps up with but also enhances your business processes.

THE SMALL BUSINESS FINANCE BIBLE

SETTING UP AND MANAGING YOUR ACCOUNTING SYSTEM

Identify the accounting method that will best suit your business needs. There are two primary methods: cash-based and accrual. Cash-based accounting is straightforward – you record transactions when cash changes hands. On the other hand, accrual-based accounting recognizes income and expenses when they are incurred, regardless of when money is exchanged. Small businesses typically choose cash-based accounting for its simplicity.

Next, it's time to decide whether to do your accounting manually or use software. While manual entry can be inexpensive, it's labor-intensive and prone to error. Accounting software, in contrast, automates many processes and ensures accuracy. It's widely recommended to opt for software.

Now that you have chosen a method and whether to go manual or digital, follow these steps:

STEP 1. OPEN A BUSINESS BANK ACCOUNT:

Separate personal finances from business transactions by opening a dedicated business bank account. This separation simplifies record-keeping and is essential for accurate financial reporting.

STEP 2. CHOOSE AN ACCOUNTING SOFTWARE:

Select software that meets the needs of your small business. Look for user-friendly interfaces, scalability as your business grows, customer support availability, and integration with other tools like point of sale systems or payment processors.

STEP 3. SET UP YOUR CHART OF ACCOUNTS:

A chart of accounts is a list of all the financial accounts—both income and expense—of the company. It provides structure to your financial reports and helps you categorize transactions. Most software comes with a default chart that can be customized to fit your specific operations.

THE SMALL BUSINESS FINANCE BIBLE

STEP 4. INPUT OPENING BALANCES:

If this isn't a brand-new business, enter opening balances from previous accounting records into the software. This serves as the starting point for all new transactions.

STEP 5. CONNECT BANK ACCOUNTS:

Many modern accounting systems allow you to synchronize with your bank account directly, which facilitates live transaction records. This feature reduces data entry time and also helps in reconciling bank statements with ease.

It's crucial now to establish ongoing management practices:

1. **Bookkeeping Routine:** Set aside regular intervals (daily or weekly) for bookkeeping tasks—recording transactions, checking cash flows, invoicing clients, and paying vendors. Consistent habits prevent backlogs that could turn into accounting nightmares.

2. **Timely Reconciliations:** Regularly reconcile checking accounts against bank statements to catch any discrepancies immediately.

3. **Tax Obligations:** Stay aware of tax deadlines specific to your business structure (sole proprietorship, partnership, LLC, etc.) and save necessary funds in a separate account if possible. Use your accounting system to generate reports that make tax filing easier.

4. **Regular Financial Reviews:** Schedule monthly financial reviews to assess the health of the business and tweak operations accordingly. Look at income statements (profit & loss), balance sheets (assets vs liabilities), and cash flow statements.

5. **Data Backup:** Ensure you have a secure backup system in place for your financial data to protect against unexpected losses due to hardware failure or cyber threats.

By following these structured steps in setting up and managing your accounting system's activity tracking feature is much more straightforward than it sounds—and its benefits pivot on arming yourself with real-time data about every aspect of your business finances. Remember not to overcomplicate things; simplicity is key in maintaining efficient small-business finance management systems that stand the test of time—and unexpected challenges alike!

THE SMALL BUSINESS FINANCE BIBLE

INTEGRATING YOUR ACCOUNTING SYSTEM WITH OTHER BUSINESS PROCESSES

One crucial aspect that often gets overlooked is the integration of your accounting system with other business processes. But worry not, as integrating doesn't have to be a complex maze; let's break it down into simple terms and understand the *'how"* and *'why'* behind this powerful synergy.

Imagine your business as a well-orchestrated orchestra: each section, from sales to inventory management, must work in harmony to create beautiful music – which in the world of business translates to profits and success. Your accounting system is akin to the conductor, setting the pace and ensuring each section follows the score accurately.

Now, let's dive into key areas where integrating your accounting system can bring substantial rewards.

1. **Sales and Invoicing**: Connecting your sales processes directly with your accounting software can shave off countless hours of manual data entry. When a sale is made, it should automatically generate an invoice, record the transaction in your books, and update your inventory all at once. This not only saves time but also reduces errors that can happen when transferring information from one place to another.

2. **Customer Relationship Management (CRM)**: Linking your CRM with accounting helps give a 360-degree view of customer interactions. Every purchase, payment, and even conversation can be tracked alongside financial data. This means you can easily identify trends, such as who are your most loyal customers or which clients tend to pay late.

3. **Inventory Management**: Goodbye to the days of physical stock takes that leave you scratching your head over discrepancies! Integrating inventory systems ensures that what you have on paper (or screen) matches what's on your shelves. When an item is sold, its count in inventory automatically updates, which in turn adjusts financial records for cost of goods sold.

4. **Payroll Systems**: By automating payroll within your integrated system, you ensure that employee payments—including taxes—are calculated correctly and timely reflected in your accounts. This not only keeps employees happy but also keeps you on good terms with tax authorities by avoiding potential filing mistakes.

5. **Expense Tracking**: Receipts piling up everywhere? By having an expense tracking system talk directly to your accounting software, receipts can be digitally stored and categorized as

soon as they're incurred. See at a glance where money is going without the tedious task of entering data line by line at month-end.

6. **E-commerce Platforms:** If you operate an online store, integration is key for real-time updates on sales activity. Orders placed online should feed directly into both inventory management and accounting systems to maintain accurate records across all platforms seamlessly.

7. **Payment Processors**: Hand-in-hand with e-commerce—or any point-of-sale system—is payment processing linkage to automatically capture sales information correctly with every swipe or click of 'purchase'.

The practicalities of these integrations come down to technology solutions that facilitate communication between different software applications used for various business functions—this is often achieved through Application Programming Interfaces (APIs).

By successfully integrating these key areas through APIs or other software solutions designed for small businesses, entrepreneurs gain access to actionable insights while enjoying increased efficiency. For example, generating reports that combine financial data with sales patterns or inventory levels can inform strategic decisions such as where to cut costs or when to invest in more stock.

Moreover, having an integrated system allows for significant time savings; freeing up precious resources that small business owners can then invest back into growing their enterprise—be it through market research, product development or simply enjoying much-needed downtime. The reality is clear: joining up your accounting system with other business processes isn't just about making life easier—it's about making your business smarter, faster and more adaptive in today's fast-paced world.

By now you should have a general understanding that integrating these different aspects of business operations isn't just helpful – it's vital for staying competitive and keeping on top of your finances without becoming overwhelmed by complexities that should be—quite frankly—straightforward affairs when equipped with the right connections.

CHAPTER 07

MANAGING CASH FLOW, BUDGETING, AND FORECASTING

THE SMALL BUSINESS FINANCE BIBLE

Cash flow is the lifeblood of any small business. Without a steady stream of cash, operations can grind to a halt, bills pile up, and the stress on the business owner can become overwhelming. To avoid cash crunches and keep the business running smoothly, it's important to master a few key techniques for managing cash effectively.

The first step in managing cash flow is understanding where your cash is coming from and where it's going. Record all cash inflows – money you receive from sales, loans, investments, and other sources. Likewise, record all outflows – expenses like rent, payroll, supplies, and loan payments. This sounds basic but can be an eye-opener once you see the patterns of your business spending.

A simple yet powerful tool to visualize your cash flow is a cash flow statement or forecast. This isn't as hard as it sounds; it is essentially a calendar that forecasts when you expect to receive cash and when your expenses will be due. Create monthly forecasts and revise them regularly as you get more information about sales and expenses.

Let's discuss some strategies you can use to ensure this stream keeps flowing positively:

1. **Invoice Promptly and Follow Up**: Your business's cash flow depends significantly on how quickly customers pay their bills. Invoice customers as soon as you deliver a product or complete a service. The sooner you send out an invoice, the sooner you're likely to get paid. Establish clear payment terms upfront and stick to them. If you allow 30 days for payment, don't let customers drag it out to 60 or 90 days.

2. **Monitor Expenses**: Keep overhead costs under control by reviewing them regularly. This doesn't necessarily mean cutting costs but managing them efficiently to ensure they're aligned with your business goals. Sometimes spending in one area can lead to savings in another or spur growth that improves cash flow long term.

3. **Maintain Cash Reserves**: Even well-managed businesses can face unexpected shortfalls due to seasonality or unforeseen expenses. A buffer of retained earnings can protect the business from having to find expensive last-minute financing solutions.

4. **Negotiate with Suppliers**: Work with suppliers to negotiate better payment terms—perhaps extending the time allowed for payments or securing bulk purchase discounts for committing to a certain volume of goods. Every penny saved here improves your cash flow.

5. **Use Technology**: There are many software tools available that help businesses manage their finances more effectively. These can automate invoicing, track expenses, monitor customer payments, and provide up-to-date reporting that helps make informed decisions faster.

THE SMALL BUSINESS FINANCE BIBLE

MONTHLY CASH FLOW FORECAST EXAMPLE			
MONTH	EXPECTED CASH INFLOW	EXPECTED CASH OUTFLOW	NET CASH FLOW
Jan	$10,000	$6,000	$4,000
Feb	$12,000	$7,500	$4,500
Mar	$8,000	$9,500	-$1,500
Apr	$14,000	$5,000	$9,000
May	$13,000	$8,200	$4,800

Note: This chart should be updated as real data comes in month-to-month.

Managing your inventory efficiently is also critical for maintaining healthy cash flow. Overstocking ties up funds unproductively; understocking may lead to missed sales opportunities which directly impact citrus flow negatively. Lastly, let's not underestimate the importance of building a good relationship with your bank or financial institution — specifically if it comes down to needing additional funds via an overdraft or loan during lean periods.

HOW TO CREATE AND MANAGE BUDGETS

Budget management is essential, not just to keep your business floating, but to also anchor it during stormy economic weathers. From micro-enterprises to substantial establishments, a well-crafted budget serves as your financial blueprint. A budget helps you to plan for future expenses and revenue, ensuring that you have enough money to keep your business running smoothly. Let's take a practical approach to budgeting that even beginners can understand and implement.

Understanding the amount of money your business generates is the foundation for building a budget. Begin by listing all sources of income. This includes sales, returns on investments, loans, and any other incomes specific to your business. Once you have this information, calculate your total monthly revenue.

THE SMALL BUSINESS FINANCE BIBLE

Now, let's break down expenses into two categories: *fixed* and *variable*. Fixed expenses are those that don't change from month to month, like rent or loan payments. Variable expenses fluctuate, such as utility bills or the cost of raw materials. List all these expenses separately.

For fixed expenses, list the actual amounts as they'll remain constant. For variable costs, look at historical data over several months to find an average. If you're just starting out, use industry benchmarks or reasonable estimates.

Here's a simple chart to illustrate how to categorize these expenses:

EXPENSE CATEGORY	EXAMPLE	TYPE
Rent	Office space lease	Fixed
Insurance	Business insurance	Fixed
Materials	Inventory purchases	Variable
Utilities	Electricity bill	Variable

Once you have your revenue and categorized expenses, it's time to create the budget. Subtract fixed and variable expenses from your total revenue. The remaining amount is either your surplus or deficit. A surplus indicates that you're bringing in more money than you're spending—a good position to be in! A deficit means you need to adjust by cutting costs or finding new income.

A budget isn't set in stone; it requires frequent revisiting and adjusting. Monitor it throughout the month, comparing actual spending against projected costs and revenue. This will alert you if certain expenses are consistently higher than expected so you can make informed decisions.

If you find your business in a deficit, consider ways to reduce costs without compromising quality or operations:

- Look for less expensive suppliers or negotiate with current ones.
- Reduce non-essential variable costs.
- Consider more cost-effective marketing strategies.

THE SMALL BUSINESS FINANCE BIBLE

No matter how well you plan, unexpected expenses can arise. That's why it's crucial to build a contingency fund into your budget. Aim for enough savings to cover at least one month of operating costs. If cutting costs isn't enough, look for ways to increase revenue:

- Introduce new products or services.
- Increase marketing efforts.
- Expand into new markets.
- Improve sales strategies.

Establish a regular review cycle—monthly is usually best—to evaluate revenue vs. expenses and adjust your budget accordingly. Examples of profitable adjustments:

1. **If utility costs are higher than expected:**
   - Consider energy-saving measures.
   - Renegotiate terms with service providers.

2. **If sales are below targets:**
   - Explore promotions to boost short-term sales.
   - Analyze market trends for product adjustments.

Creating and managing budgets doesn't have to be complex. With clear categorization of incomes and expenses and regular reviews/adjustments, you can maintain financial health for your small business. Remember that budget management is an ongoing process that can lead you toward economic stability and growth if performed diligently and smartly.

FORECASTING FUTURE FINANCIAL PERFORMANCE

Forecasting the financial performance of a small business is like trying to predict the weather for your week ahead. You look at patterns, take note of current conditions, and use tools to help give you the best guess. In doing so, you can prepare for what might come your way. For a small business, effective financial forecasting is crucial as it enables you to anticipate profits, manage cash flow and guide your business towards sustainable growth.

THE SMALL BUSINESS FINANCE BIBLE

Understanding how to forecast effectively begins with knowing your numbers - that's your starting point. From there, it's about using those numbers to map out where you are headed.

STEP 1. ANALYZE HISTORICAL DATA:

Your past financial statements are the groundwork of any good forecast. Start by reviewing your income statements, balance sheets, and cash flow statements from at least the past year. Look for trends in your revenues, costs, and profits. How does your business perform across different seasons? Are there certain products or services that are more profitable than others? These insights provide a foundation for predicting future performance.

STEP 2. KNOW YOUR DRIVERS:

Every business has key drivers that influence financial outcomes – they might be the number of customers, the average sale per customer, or cost per unit. Identify these drivers and how they have impacted your historical financial data. Understanding these will allow you to make informed assumptions about how these drivers will perform in the future.

STEP 3. CREATE SALES FORECASTS:

Sales forecasting can be daunting but vitally important. Based on historical data and considering factors such as market trends, upcoming marketing efforts, or new products, estimate your future sales volumes. Always aim for realism; being overly optimistic can be as harmful as being overly pessimistic.

STEP 4. ESTIMATE COSTS AND EXPENSES:

Just like sales, you need an accurate estimate of future costs and expenses to ensure profitability. Fixed costs such as rent or salaries will not change much. However, variable costs such as materials or shipping might fluctuate; so take into account any expected changes—maybe a supplier has announced a price increase or you're planning to expand operations.

THE SMALL BUSINESS FINANCE BIBLE

STEP 5. CONSIDER CAPITAL EXPENDITURES:

Investment in new equipment or property should also be factored into your financial forecast. Such purchases often involve significant amounts of money and can impact both cash flow and depreciation expenses over time.

STEP 6. ASSESS CASH FLOW:

The lifeblood of any small business is its cash flow – it needs to keep flowing for the business to remain healthy. Your sales and expenses forecasting should lead naturally into assessing when money will actually enter or leave your bank account.

STEP 7. PLAN FOR DIFFERENT SCENARIOS:

It's wise to prepare not just one forecast but several, covering best-case, worst-case, and most likely scenarios. Doing this creates a sensitivity analysis which helps you understand how changes in key variables may impact your financial health.

STEP 8. DRAFT YOUR PROJECTIONS:

With all this data at hand, draft up monthly or quarterly projections for at least the next year if not further out. This timetable allows for regular review against actual performance enabling timely adjustments to be made.

STEP 9. REVIEW REGULARLY:

A forecast isn't something you create once then shelve away forever – it's a dynamic tool that needs regular updating as real-world events unfold. Set aside time each month to compare actual results with projections to understand where things are on/off track.

THE SMALL BUSINESS FINANCE BIBLE

Remember that accuracy in forecasting comes from understanding both historical performance and present conditions while keeping an eye on future possibilities through educated assumptions based on data-driven analyses. By following these steps methodically, you can build a robust forecast that will guide management decisions and help pave the way for long-term success in your small business venture.

CHAPTER 08

LOANS, INVESTMENTS, AND EQUITY FINANCING

THE SMALL BUSINESS FINANCE BIBLE

Entrepreneurs often encounter the challenge of securing capital to start or grow their business. Understanding the different sources of business capital is crucial for making informed decisions. Below, we'll explore three fundamental avenues: loans, investments, and equity financing.

1. Loans: A loan is a sum of money that a person or entity borrows from a lender with the agreement to pay back the principal amount along with interest over a predetermined period. For small businesses, this source of capital is conventional and comes in various forms, including bank loans, lines of credit, and Small Business Administration (SBA) loans. Bank loans are usually the first option business owners think about. They involve borrowing a pre-set amount of money to be paid back with interest via monthly payments. The banks may require collateral against the loan as security for repayment and will assess a business's creditworthiness before lending.

A line of credit provides more flexibility, allowing businesses to borrow up to a certain limit and only pay interest on the portion used. This option is especially handy for managing cash flow fluctuations or unexpected expenses. SBA loans are partially guaranteed by the U.S. Small Business Administration and are designed to assist small businesses that may not qualify for traditional bank loans. They tend to have lower down payments and longer repayment terms but also involve an extensive application process.

2. Investments: Investments involve obtaining capital from investors who provide cash in exchange for becoming part-owners or shareholders in your business. This can occur at various stages, ranging from seed funding for new startups to larger rounds of financing for established companies looking to expand.

Angel investors are typically affluent individuals who offer capital in exchange for equity or convertible debt in startups with high growth potential. Angel investing is risky but can also provide valuable mentorship and industry connections.

Venture capitalists (VCs) represent funds or firms that invest in young, emerging companies which demonstrate high growth potential. In exchange for substantial sums of capital, VCs often demand significant control over company decisions and a substantial share of future profits. Crowdfunding has emerged as an alternative investment avenue through platforms like Kickstarter or Indiegogo. Here, entrepreneurs present their idea to a broad audience and raise small amounts of money from many backers, often rewarding them with early access to products or equity in return.

THE SMALL BUSINESS FINANCE BIBLE

3. Equity Financing: Equity financing involves raising capital by selling shares of your company's stock. Unlike a loan, it does not have to be repaid; instead, investors gain ownership stakes in the hopes that they will earn returns when the company grows and becomes more valuable.

Public stock offerings are one way for large companies to raise equity by selling shares on public stock exchanges — process known as Initial Public Offering (IPO). However, this route is complex and regulatory-intensive, making it less viable for small businesses. Private placements are more accessible for smaller enterprises whereby shares are sold directly to individual investors such as venture capitalists or angel investors without making a public offering.

Each method has its own set of advantages and trade-offs that must be carefully considered based on the specific needs and situation of your business.

SOURCE	PROS	CONS
Loans	Fixed repayment plan	Requires collateral; interest payments
	Predictable monthly payments	Strict eligibility criteria
	May improve credit score	
Investments	Large sums possible	Dilution of ownership
	Access to investor expertise	High expectations for growth
	No repayment obligation	Giving up some control
Equity Financing	No debt incurred	Permanent dilution of ownership
	Long-term investor commitment	Sharing future profits
	No repayments	Complex regulatory requirements

Selecting the right mix or single source of capital requires evaluating your business's goals, risk tolerance, current financial situation, industry trends, and long-term strategic plans. By understanding these key forms of business capital, you position yourself on a firmer footing when seeking funding for your entrepreneurial journey.

THE SMALL BUSINESS FINANCE BIBLE

THE IMPACT OF DEBT AND EQUITY ON FINANCIAL STATEMENTS

As a small business owner, maintaining a strong financial health is crucial. One aspect that often leads to confusion is the impact of debt and equity on a business's financial statements. When a company borrows money, whether it is from a bank loan or issuing bonds, this is registered as a liability on the balance sheet. Why so? Because this money must be paid back over time. On your balance sheet, you will notice things like *"long-term debt"* or *"notes payable,"* and these are just fancier terms for the amounts you owe.

Now, what happens when you take on debt? Initially, when the loan hits your account, your cash on hand increases — showing up in the assets section of the balance sheet. It might give the impression that your business is flush with money, but remember, since there's an equal increase in liabilities (the loan amount), your overall equity doesn't change at this point.

Debt impacts another part of your financials — the income statement. The cost of borrowing, known as interest expense, appears here. Regular payments to reduce the loan principal don't get featured here; instead, they reflect back on the balance sheet by decreasing the liability over time. However, that interest payment is different because it's categorized as an expense due to its nature of being a cost of financing.

Let's shift gears to equity financing now. This is when you finance your business by selling shares to investors. From sole proprietorships to partnerships and corporations, all can have some form of equity even though they may be expressed differently across each type of business structure.

When you issue equity, say by selling stock in a corporation, you receive cash or other assets, boosting assets on your balance sheet without boosting liabilities since there's no obligation to repay investors their initial investment; rather they get ownership in the company proportional to their investment. Sounds straightforward? Here's where it gets interesting: the owners' equity or shareholders' equity section on the balance sheet grows because you've essentially traded a piece of your business for that cash or asset boost.

The promising side of using equity over debt financing lies in not having any required payments like interest that would affect your income statement regularly. However, it means sharing profits with shareholders when distributing dividends and also sharing decision-making power depending on how much control investors gain through their shares.

THE SMALL BUSINESS FINANCE BIBLE

One intriguing point about incorporating both debt and equity into your financing strategy is their impact on leverage and profitability ratios, commonly used indicators to compute financial health and performance. For instance, taking up more debt can improve certain profitability ratios as long as earnings exceed the cost of debt but beware – too much debt can also signal riskiness to potential lenders or investors examining your financial statements.

Owners' contributions and draws are significant movements within equity too but are mostly seen in non-corporate businesses like sole proprietorships or partnerships where owners may invest personal funds (contributions) into their businesses or withdraw funds (draws) for personal use. These transactions adjust the owners' capital accounts located in the equity section rather than operating revenues or expenses affecting net income directly.

One must realize proper management between leveraging debt and cultivating equity is not just analytical but strategic too. The decisions echo through every corner of your financial statements – from utilizing resources efficiently to ensuring flexibility for future growth opportunities.

STRATEGIES FOR FINANCING GROWTH

One of the critical components of scaling your small business resides in savvy financing choices that align with your long-term objectives. Below are pragmatic strategies for financing growth while maintaining the inherent simplicity needed for clear understanding and actionable insights.

1. Profits as a Foundation: Before seeking external avenues of finance, consider utilizing retained earnings – the surplus profit you reinvest into your business after all expenses, including dividends, are paid out. Such internally generated funds are interest-free and void of repayment pressures, making them a solid foundation for funding growth at your own pace. It's like using the fruits of your business's success to feed its future endeavors.

2. Understanding Loans and Credit: Debt is a commonly treaded path for financing expansion. Banks and credit unions offer varied loan products tailored to small businesses. A term loan provides a lump sum that you repay with interest over a specified period. Such loans suit heavy, one-time investments in equipment or property. Alternatively, if you anticipate periodic expenses, a line of credit might better serve your needs. It operates much like a credit card – you draw funds up to your limit as needed and only pay interest on the amount used. This flexibility can be particularly

THE SMALL BUSINESS FINANCE BIBLE

beneficial for managing cash flow during growth phases. When considering debt options, remember to evaluate the cost of borrowing—the interest rate and any additional fees—and ensure that the growth anticipated from the investment can service this debt.

3. Venturing into Equity: Exchanging financial injection for ownership stakes—equity—can offer significant capital without repayment stress. Attracting investors or new partners generally involves diluting ownership but can bring invaluable resources, including funds, expertise, and networks essential to scaling your business.

Angel investors typically support startups with deep pockets and mentorship opportunities, but they seek substantial returns on their investments. Meanwhile, venture capitalists (VCs) may offer larger sums of money but often come in at later stages than angels and require persuasive evidence of future profitability.

4. Crowdfunding: Recent years have seen an uptick in crowdfunding popularity where you pitch your business idea or project online via platforms like Kickstarter or Indiegogo. This method allows masses of people to contribute financially towards your goal in exchange for some reward—maybe early access to products or exclusive perks. Crowdfunding not only secures capital but also validates your business concept through public interest, creating a base of supporters who may become future clients.

5. Government Grants & Subsidies: Keep an eye on government initiatives aiming to bolster small businesses. Grants and subsidies are akin to financial windfalls since they generally don't demand repayment or equity stakes and often come with added support services—be it training programs or networking events. Eligibility typically depends on meeting certain criteria such as industry type, size of the company, or intended use of funds.

6. Strategic Alliances & Business Relationships: Sometimes overlooked yet potentially powerful is leveraging business relationships for mutual gain. You may form strategic alliances with complementary companies – this could involve cross-promotions or joint ventures that economize on expenses while broadening market reach. Barter arrangements can also lessen capital outlays—trading goods or services with other businesses preserves cash for other growth-critical needs.

THE SMALL BUSINESS FINANCE BIBLE

Growth financing need not be shrouded in complexity. By leveraging these strategies—from reinvesting profits to engaging new investors—you lay down economic stepping stones towards scalable expansion while remaining vigilant over costs and risks involved.

Remember that each strategy possesses its pros and cons; a mix optimized for your unique circumstances usually works best. Diligent research coupled with foresight will gear up any small business owner to harness their desired path for capitalizing expansion efficiently and effectively.

CHAPTER

09

UNDERSTANDING FINANCIAL STATEMENTS

THE SMALL BUSINESS FINANCE BIBLE

BALANCE SHEETS, INCOME STATEMENTS, AND CASH FLOW STATEMENTS

When you're running a small business, it's not just about the product you sell or the service you offer. It's also about keeping your business financially healthy. To do that, you need to understand three key financial statements: the balance sheet, income statement, and cash flow statement.

A *balance sheet* is a snapshot of your business's financial condition at a specific moment in time. It shows what you own (assets), what you owe (liabilities), and what's left over for you and any other owners (equity). Think of it as a quick summary of your business's financial bookkeeping up to that point.

Why is a balance sheet important? It helps you quickly see if your assets are enough to cover your liabilities, which can tell you about the overall health of your business. For instance, if liabilities outweigh assets, that might indicate potential trouble ahead. On the other hand, if the equation tips the other way, your business likely sits on a stable foundation.

Next up is the *income statement*, also known as a profit and loss statement. This document shows how much money your business made and spent over a period - typically over a quarter or year. The income statement lists all revenue streams and subtracts expenses to show net income or loss for that period. The income statement is crucial because it shows whether or not your business is profitable. If you're making more than you're spending, that's good news! You're operating at a profit. However, if it's the other way around, it might be time to re-evaluate expenses, pricing strategies or look for ways to boost sales.

Lastly, we've got the *cash flow statement*. Cash is king in business; without it, things come grinding to a halt – no matter how profitable your company might appear on paper. This statement records when money actually enters or exits your bank account from operations, investing, and financing activities. This is especially important for small businesses because it can highlight liquidity problems that aren't obvious from just looking at the balance sheet and income statement. Positive cash flow means you have more cash coming in than going out – it's like having healthy blood pressure for a person – while negative cash flow is cause for concern.

THE SMALL BUSINESS FINANCE BIBLE

Understanding how these three financial statements work together gives you full insight into your business's financial health:

- 💵 The balance sheet provides an overview of the current standing of assets versus liabilities.
- 💵 The income statement shows operational effectiveness by detailing profit or loss.
- 💵 The cash flow statement reveals how well cash resources are being managed and helps predict future liquidity challenges.

All three documents serve as essential tools for making informed decisions about investments, budgeting, cost-cutting measures, and predicting future performance. For successful management of a small enterprise, learning to read these financial statements isn't just beneficial - it's vital. They will guide decisions such as when to expand operations or tighten spending belts - savvy moves that could either save or propel your business forward.

HOW TO READ AND INTERPRET THESE DOCUMENTS

Understanding balance sheets, income statements, and cash flow statements is as crucial as knowing the ingredients in your favorite recipe. Without recognizing what each figure and term means, it's almost impossible to gauge the financial health of your business accurately. Here's a simple guide to help you read and interpret these documents:

To interpret a **balance sheet**, start by examining the assets side. Assets are often listed in order of liquidity, meaning how quickly they can be converted into cash. Current assets, such as cash and inventory, are expected to be used or sold within a year. Long-term assets include equipment and property. Liabilities follow a similar structure. Current liabilities, like accounts payable or short-term loans, are due within a year, while long-term liabilities may consist of mortgages or deferred tax liabilities. The golden rule for reading balance sheets is this: assets should ideally equal the sum of liabilities plus equity. The equity portion represents what the owners truly 'own' – the net worth of the business.

How do you know if your balance sheet looks good? A fundamental measure is comparing current assets (cash or items easily converted to cash within a year) against current liabilities (debts due within a year). This measure is known as the current ratio and is calculated as:

THE SMALL BUSINESS FINANCE BIBLE

> **Current Ratio = Current Assets / Current Liabilities**

A ratio above 1 indicates that you have more assets than liabilities due soon – a sign of liquidity.

Now let's move on to the **income statement**. The top line shows revenue – money coming in from sales before any costs are deducted. As you move down, various types of expenses are subtracted such as cost of goods sold (COGS), operating expenses, taxes, etc., until we reach the bottom line – net income. Keep an eye out for trends here; increasing net income over time suggests your business is growing more profitable. Conversely, a decrease might signal trouble that needs addressing. Profit margins also offer insight:

> **Gross Profit Margin = (Revenue - COGS) / Revenue**
>
> **Operating Profit Margin = Operating Income / Revenue**
>
> **Net Profit Margin = Net Income / Revenue**

Margins allow you to see efficiency in different areas: gross profit margin reveals how well you manage direct costs linked to production or service delivery; operating profit margin reflects overhead control; net profit margin indicates overall profitability after all expenses.

Lastly, remember that profitability does not equal cash flow. This brings us to the **cash flow statement**, which is categorized into three sections: *operations, investing*, and *financing activities*. Operations show the cash generated from normal business operations; investing details cash used for investments like property or equipment; financing shows money exchanged between the company and its owners or creditors.

Positive operational cash flow signals your core business activities are generating adequate funds. Watch out for big discrepancies between net income and cash generated from operations – it could indicate accounting irregularities or issues with collecting payments.

A valuable tool here is the free cash flow calculation:

> **Free Cash Flow = Operating Cash Flow - Capital Expenditures**

THE SMALL BUSINESS FINANCE BIBLE

It shows how much cash you have left after maintaining or expanding assets. It's a good measure of business health – consistent positive values suggest you're in good shape to pay debts, reinvest in your business, and weather downturns.

So, when reviewing these documents:

- Check if your assets cover liabilities on your balance sheet.
- Evaluate revenue trends and profit margins on your income statement.
- Analyze operational cash flow on your cash flow statement to understand liquidity.
- Use ratios like current ratio and free cash flow for more nuanced insights.

As an exercise: Calculate the Current Ratio and Free Cash Flow for your business using the simplified financial data below:

ABC Company Simplified Financial Data

- Current Assets: $150k
- Current Liabilities: $100k
- Operating Cash Flow: $80k
- Capital Expenditures: $20k

Once you've calculated your Current Ratio and Free Cash Flow, answer the following questions:

1. Does the ABC Company have more assets than liabilities due soon?
2. Is ABC Company generating enough cash from its core business activities after maintaining or expanding its assets?

Provide your calculations along with answers for the questions.

Answer Explanation:

To calculate the Current Ratio:

> **Current Ratio = Current Assets / Current Liabilities**

Based on the ABC Company's financial data:

$$\text{Current Ratio} = \$150k / \$100k = 1.5$$

This means that for every dollar of liability due within a year, ABC Company has $1.50 in assets easily convertible to cash, which means they have more assets than liabilities due soon, answering question 1 positively.

Now, to calculate the Free Cash Flow:

$$\text{Free Cash Flow} = \text{Operating Cash Flow} - \text{Capital Expenditures}$$

Based on the ABC Company's financial data:

$$\text{Free Cash Flow} = \$80k - \$20k = \$60k$$

ABC Company has a positive free cash flow, which indicates that they are generating sufficient cash from their core operations after accounting for the costs of maintaining or expanding their assets. This provides a positive answer to question 2 as well. ABC Company appears to have a healthy liquidity position with more current assets than current liabilities and a strong ability to generate cash from its business operations after covering capital expenditures.

COMMON PITFALLS IN FINANCIAL ANALYSIS

Financial analysis is a key component of running a successful small business. It helps you understand where your business stands and guides your decision-making process. However, it's not without its challenges. Many small business owners fall into traps that can skew their financial analysis, leading to poor decisions and potentially harming their business's health.

One of the most prevalent issues is *not having a clear objective for the analysis*. Without a specific goal in mind, it's easy to become overwhelmed by the sheer volume of data available. You must ask yourself what you want to achieve with your analysis. Are you looking to identify cost-cutting opportunities, understand revenue trends, or evaluate investment options? A focused approach will yield more meaningful insights.

THE SMALL BUSINESS FINANCE BIBLE

Another trap many fall into is *overlooking the importance of context*. Numbers on a spreadsheet don't tell the full story if they aren't considered within the broader economic, industry-specific, or seasonal landscape. For instance, a dip in sales might seem alarming at first glance but could be normal for your industry after the holiday season. Similarly, a single high-performing month might not signify a positive trend if it was due to a one-off event.

Reliance on outdated or inaccurate information can also lead to misguided conclusions. In the fast-paced environment of small business operations, it's vital to work with the most current data available. Utilizing information that is weeks or months old could lead you to make decisions that don't align with your current financial situation.

One subtle yet significant mistake is *confirmation bias*—analyzing financial data in a way that supports preconceived notions or desired results instead of taking an objective view. A business owner may want so badly to see growth that they interpret any positive number as an unquestionable sign of success, overlooking data that might suggest caution or further investigation.

Overcomplicating analysis can also be problematic. While advanced financial models and statistical techniques have their place, they can be confusing and unnecessary for many small business needs. Simplicity often leads to better understanding and clearer action steps; thus, using straightforward methods can be more effective for day-to-day business finance management.

Conversely, *oversimplifying your analysis* can be just as detrimental as overcomplicating it. Some might choose only to look at net profit each month without considering other important factors like cash flow, debt levels, or inventory turnover rates. These additional metrics can give more depth and accuracy to your financial picture.

In doing financial analysis, it's essential to *avoid underestimating expenses*—a common pitfall that can throw off your entire budgeting process. It's easy for small expenses to slip through unnoticed or for variable costs like utilities or materials prices to increase unexpectedly. Be sure always to add some buffer in your expense forecasts for unforeseen costs.

Ignoring non-financial factors that affect financial health is another oversight often made by small business owners. Customer satisfaction levels, employee morale, and operational efficiencies have considerable impacts on a company's finances but might not show up directly on balance sheets or

P&L statements. Additionally, many businesses fail by *not regularly performing financial analysis*—or only doing so when there seems to be an issue. Waiting until problems arise means missing out on opportunities for improvement and growth that could have been identified with consistent monitoring.

Finally, overlooking debts and liabilities can lead to an overly optimistic view of your business's finances. While focusing on assets and revenue streams is natural and important, understanding and managing debts is just as crucial.

Avoiding these common pitfalls in financial analysis isn't just about protecting your company; it's about laying down the groundwork for long-term success and stability. By having clear objectives, considering context, using up-to-date information, maintaining objectivity, keeping methods manageable without oversimplifying them, expecting expenses accurately considering non-financial influences undertaking regular reviews, and being mindful of debt responsibilities—you'll be well-equipped to perform meaningful financial analyses that drive smart business decisions.

CHAPTER 10

ADVANCED ACCOUNTING TECHNIQUES

THE SMALL BUSINESS FINANCE BIBLE

INTERNAL CONTROLS FOR PREVENTING FRAUD

Internal controls are procedures and policies put in place by a business to ensure the validity and accuracy of its financial statements, improve operational efficiency, and reduce the risk of fraud. Effective internal controls can help prevent various types of fraud, including asset misappropriation, corruption, and financial statement fraud.

One key aspect of internal controls is segregation of duties. This means dividing responsibilities among different employees so that no single individual has control over all aspects of a financial transaction. For example, one person should handle cash receipts while another manages record-keeping. By doing this, it becomes more challenging for any individual to commit and conceal fraud.

Another effective control mechanism is the implementation of an authorization procedure. Significant transactions should require approval from a higher authority within the company. Similarly, new vendors or changes in banking information should undergo scrutiny before being processed. This can prevent unauthorized or falsified transactions from slipping through unnoticed.

Regular accounting reconciliations are also crucial. Reconciling bank statements with book entries monthly helps identify discrepancies that could indicate errors or fraudulent activity. If discrepancies are found, they can be investigated immediately. The use of physical controls should not be overlooked either. Locked storage for sensitive documents, controlled access to inventory areas, and surveillance cameras can deter misappropriation of assets. Additionally, consider using tamper-evident seals on products or storage units to provide an extra layer of security.

Implementing an effective reporting system also plays a vital role in preventing fraud. This includes setting up mechanisms through which employees can report suspected fraudulent activities anonymously without fear of retribution. A clear policy that emphasizes zero tolerance towards fraud should be communicated to all employees.

Small businesses often overlook external audits due to their costs; however, they serve as an essential component in detecting and deterring fraud. Having an independent auditor review your books annually brings a fresh set of eyes onto your finances and can reveal irregularities you may have missed.

Let's look at a practical example involving inventory theft prevention using internal controls: A small retail store begins noticing discrepancies in its inventory levels where occasional stock seems to vanish without any sales records. To counteract this issue, the store implements several control measures:

1. **Access Control:** Only authorized personnel receive keys to the inventory storage room.
2. **Segregation of Duties:** Different employees are responsible for ordering stock (Purchasing), receiving stock (Receiving), and managing stock levels (Inventory Management).
3. **Reconciliation:** The Inventory Manager periodically compares actual stock levels with recorded entries.
4. **Surveillance:** Cameras installed in storage areas monitor activities during and after business hours.
5. **Inventory Audits:** Regular unannounced inventory audits are conducted by an external party.

Through these steps, the store successfully deters internal theft as it becomes far more difficult for individuals to steal without detection.

Internal controls serve as a fortress guarding your business's assets and reputation from the potential onslaught of fraudulent activities. Your small business might feel immune to such risks—but take heed; fraudsters often prey on this complacency. By setting up robust internal control systems tailored to your specific needs and regularly reviewing these controls for effectiveness, you actively participate in fortifying your business against financial malfeasance.

TIME-SAVING AUTOMATION IN ACCOUNTING PRACTICES

Traditionally, accounting has been a labor-intensive activity, with professionals often burdened by repetitive tasks such as data entry, reconciling transactions, and generating reports. However, with the advent of automation in accounting practices, these activities are becoming more efficient. Automation software now has the capability to handle routine tasks quickly and with fewer errors than manual processing.

One notable technique is the use of *automated data entry tools*. These tools can connect to bank accounts and credit cards to automatically import transactions into an accounting system. This not only saves time that would be spent manually entering data but also reduces the likelihood of errors that can occur when manually inputting vast amounts of financial information.

THE SMALL BUSINESS FINANCE BIBLE

A practical example includes cloud-based accounting platforms like *QuickBooks Online* or *Xero*. These platforms offer direct feeds from banks and credit card companies so transactions flow automatically into your books. Imagine a chart where manual entries per day drop from hours to nearly zero as automation takes over—this is the reality provided by these tools.

Another significant advancement is in invoice processing. The days of manually creating invoices, sending them out, and then tracking payments are dwindling thanks to automation. Today's software platforms can generate invoices based on preset information, send reminders for payments, and even match received payments against outstanding invoices automatically.

Consider Amy's Craft Supplies: she uses a software solution that auto-generates invoices based on customer orders. The system sends out payment reminder emails and updates her records as soon as payment goes through her bank – all without lifting a finger after the initial setup.

In addition to managing incoming funds, automated expense tracking can vastly improve how outgoings are handled. By connecting credit card and bank statements directly into accounting software, expenses are categorized as they happen, laying out a clear picture of spending without manual intervention. A line graph representing expenditure over time could now be automatically updated every month, providing instant visibility for businesses.

Payroll processing is another area where automation has saved immense amounts of time for small businesses. Activities like calculating pay, deducting taxes, and distributing employee paychecks have become automated largely due to modern payroll software solutions that are intuitive and user-friendly.

Let's take a bakery shop; instead of calculating working hours and tax deductions for each employee by hand every fortnight, they opt for an automated payroll system that computes everything once employee details are imputed. The result? An error-free payroll process completed within minutes instead of hours.

Also noteworthy is tax preparation, which used to be one of the most time-consuming tasks in accounting. With up-to-date financial data at their fingertips courtesy of automatic recording throughout the year, accountants can prepare tax filings much more quickly and accurately.

Reporting too has been revolutionized by automation; custom reports on financial health no longer require extensive manual manipulation of data points. Dashboards provided by accounting software give real-time insights at a glance – often customizable so that a small business owner can see exactly what they need without digging through spreadsheets or compiling figures themselves.

Finally, let's consider compliance checks which are essential but often complex parts of accounting practices; automations help here as well. With systems programmed to stay abreast of regulatory changes and identify any discrepancies or red flags within financial records instantly eliminates concerns over potential non-compliance that could lead to fines or penalties.

RATIO ANALYSIS FOR PERFORMANCE EVALUATION

Ratio analysis stands as one of the stalwarts in advanced accounting techniques, offering deep insights into a company's financial health and operational efficiency. Understanding ratio analysis provides business owners, managers, and stakeholders with a critical tool for performance evaluation.

It involves comparing different figures from the balance sheet, income statement, and cash flow statement to yield quantifiable measures of a company's performance. These comparisons can provide crucial indicators of financial stability or distress.

There are several key categories of ratios used in performance evaluation:

1. **Liquidity Ratios:** These ratios determine how well a company can meet its short-term obligations with its current assets. The most common liquidity ratios include the Current Ratio and Quick Ratio.

2. **Profitability Ratios:** These help assess a company's ability to generate earnings as compared to its expenses and other costs. Profitability ratios include Gross Margin Ratio, Operating Margin Ratio, and Net Profit Margin.

3. **Leverage Ratios:** These indicate the extent to which a company is financed by debt and its ability to meet financial obligations. They include ratios such as Debt-to-Equity Ratio and Interest Coverage Ratio.

4. **Efficiency Ratios:** Efficiency ratios measure how well a company utilizes its assets and manages its operations. Inventory Turnover Ratio and Accounts Receivable Turnover Ratio are prominent examples.

THE SMALL BUSINESS FINANCE BIBLE

5. **Market Value Ratios:** These are used to evaluate the investment potential of the company's stocks, including the Price/Earnings Ratio and Market/Book Ratio.

To illustrate ratio analysis in action, let's take an example of a fictional small business named *"TechGadgets,"* which sells electronic devices.

TECHGADGETS' SELECTED FINANCIAL INFORMATION:

ITEM	VALUE
Current Assets	$150,000
Current Liabilities	$100,000
Total Equity	$200,000
Net Sales	$500,000
Cost of Goods Sold (COGS)	$300,000
Operating Expenses	$100,000
Interest Expense	$20,000
Net Income	$80,000

Using these values, we can calculate some key ratios:

1. Current Ratio = Current Assets / Current Liabilities
 = $150,000 / $100,000
 = 1.5

A current ratio greater than 1 indicates that TechGadgets has more current assets than liabilities—a good sign of liquidity.

2. Gross Margin Ratio = (Net Sales - COGS) / Net Sales
 = ($500,000 - $300,000) / $500,000
 = 0.4 or 40%

This suggests that for every dollar TechGadgets makes in sales, it retains 40 cents as gross profit before other expenses are deducted.

3. Debt-to-Equity Ratio = Total Liabilities / Total Equity

If TechGadgets has total liabilities of $250,000 including current liabilities:

$$= \$250{,}000 / \$200{,}000$$
$$= 1.25$$

This would suggest that TechGadgets uses $1.25 in debt for every dollar of equity—potentially indicating moderate leverage.

Through analyzing these ratios over time or in comparison to industry standards or competitors', TechGadgets can draw insights about their financial stability and efficiency:

- 💵 A decreasing trend in the current ratio could signify worsening liquidity.
- 💵 A disparity between gross margin ratio of TechGadgets and industry average might indicate potential issues in pricing or cost control.
- 💵 An increasing debt-to-equity ratio could show over-reliance on borrowing which may increase financial risk.

While each ratio provides valuable information on its own, it is through their collective assessment that business owners derive actionable insights. In doing so however they must consider external factors such as economic conditions or changes in consumer preferences which might influence performance measures indirectly.

In applying this knowledge practically to small businesses such as "TechGadgets", owners can make data-driven decisions regarding operations –e.g., adjusting credit terms or improving inventory management processes– ultimately enhancing overall business performance.

PART III

BOOKKEEPING FOR SMALL BUSINESS

THE SMALL BUSINESS FINANCE BIBLE

Bookkeeping may appear daunting, but it is the cornerstone of a prosperous business structure. Here, we simplify the maze of record-keeping into understandable and actionable strategies. We start by introducing you to setting up your system—whether you lean towards time-tested traditional methods or cutting-edge digital solutions, we've got you covered. Next, we unveil the secrets of maintaining impeccable records. You'll learn how to organize receipts, invoices, and other financial documents effectively. Our aim is to ensure that when it comes to archival and retrieval, your documentation is as orderly as they come.

You'll gain insights into navigating payroll complexities, extending employee benefits, and working seamlessly with independent contractors—equipping you with the knowledge to handle personnel finances smoothly. Moving forward, engaging in periodic reviews and reconciliations doesn't just catch issues; it prevents them. We focus on how regular checkups can keep your finances in mint condition throughout the year.

Finally, we highlight how strategic use of bookkeeping data can elevate your business decisions. By analyzing costs versus benefits and adapting your approach as your enterprise expands, you will be able not only to sustain but also spur growth in your business. Prepare to transform your bookkeeping from an administrative task into a strategic asset that guides your business journey!

CHAPTER 11

BASICS OF BOOKKEEPING

THE SMALL BUSINESS FINANCE BIBLE

Understanding the basic premise behind bookkeeping and integrating it effectively into your business practices can be a transformative tool for small business owners. Bookkeeping isn't just about complying with legal requirements; it's a fundamental component that can carve the path to financial clarity and long-term success. ookkeeping is the regular recording of a company's financial transactions. It's the process of documenting income, expenses, assets, and liabilities in a systematic manner. This practice enables business owners to see their financial situation at all times. Although it might seem like a mundane task, proper bookkeeping can keep your business on track financially.

Imagine owning a small local bakery. Each day you buy ingredients, sell baked goods, pay utility bills, handle payroll for your staff, and perhaps occasionally replace or repair equipment. Every dollar spent or received must be accounted for.

Effective bookkeeping in this scenario would involve recording all these transactions diligently. This way you would know how much money is being spent on ingredients and what products are bringing in the most income. It could show you that although croissants are popular, they are not necessarily profitable due to their high production costs.

Maintaining accurate records through bookkeeping also helps during tax season. All businesses must pay taxes, and with organized financial records, it becomes much less tedious to report income and claim permissible deductions. This organization effectively could save the bakery precious resources by avoiding overpayment on taxes or penalties for underpayment.

Moreover, well-kept books can be invaluable when seeking financial assistance or investors for your business. When lenders or investors ask for your business's financial statements, they want to see clear evidence of your company's financial health and potential for profitability. A bakery that desires to expand will need to present detailed accounts showing strong sales figures and controlled expenses to secure a loan successfully.

In addition to external utility, bookkeeping also plays an internal role in aiding decision-making. By systematically recording each transaction, you build up data over time. This data analysis could reveal trends such as seasonal increases in turnover or unnecessary recurring expenses that could be cut down. Our bakery owner might notice that the sale of cookies peaks around holidays and choose to boost production during these periods while decreasing cookie production when demand is low.

THE SMALL BUSINESS FINANCE BIBLE

One vital aspect of bookkeeping is creating a budget for your business operations. A budget acts as a blueprint for how your business intends to spend its resources over a given period. With solid bookkeeping practices in place, building an accurate budget becomes easier because past expenses and revenues serve as valuable benchmarks.

This process also ties into cash flow management—the ebb and flow of cash in and out of your business bank account. Understanding this cycle through effective bookkeeping helps ensure that there's enough cash on hand to pay bills when they're due while optimizing the timing of income and expenses so that liquidity issues never arise.

Small businesses should avoid thinking of bookkeeping as merely ticking boxes for compliance purposes alone but view it as an essential instrument in their toolkit—a form of empowerment through information that fosters informed decision-making.

While software solutions make bookkeeping more manageable than ever, it remains important not to rely solely on them without understanding what the numbers mean for your unique situation. Our bakery owner may use accounting software but still needs to comprehend her shop's specific financial dynamics—like tracking inventory waste or identifying her most profitable catering opportunities.

SETTING UP A BOOKKEEPING SYSTEM: TRADITIONAL VS. DIGITAL OPTIONS

When running a small business, one of the most crucial aspects to ensure its financial health is setting up a solid bookkeeping system. Bookkeeping involves recording and tracking all financial transactions, including sales, purchases, and payments. There are two primary bookkeeping systems to consider: traditional and digital.

Traditional bookkeeping has been around for centuries. It typically involves physical books or ledgers, where financial transactions are recorded manually with a pen and paper. This system requires meticulous attention to detail and a good understanding of accounting principles.

To set up a traditional bookkeeping system, follow these steps:

1. Purchase accounting ledgers or journals.
2. Determine your accounting method (cash or accrual).

3. Organize your source documents (receipts, invoices).
4. Record transactions daily in the journal.
5. Post summary totals to the general ledger.
6. Reconcile accounts monthly.
7. Prepare financial statements quarterly and annually.

While traditional methods have their charm, digital options have become increasingly popular due to their convenience and efficiency. Digital bookkeeping uses software to record financial transactions on the computer or in the cloud.

Here's how to set up a digital system:

1. Choose bookkeeping software that fits your business needs.
2. Set up an account and customize the settings for your business structure.
3. Connect your bank accounts and sync transactions automatically.
4. Categorize expenses as they appear in real-time.
5. Use the software reporting features to analyze financial data.
6. Back-up your data regularly for security purposes.

Both these systems have their pros and cons which are outlined below in a simple chart:

CRITERIA	TRADITIONAL BOOKKEEPING	DIGITAL BOOKKEEPING
Initial Setup	Inexpensive; requires ledgers	Cost of software
Accessibility	Accessible anytime	Requires computer/internet
Data Entry	Manual entry	Automated syncing
Accuracy	Error-prone manual calculations	Reduced errors with automation
Report Generation	Time-consuming	Quick and customizable
Data Backup	Physically copying papers	Automatic online backups
Scalability	Difficult to scale	Easily scalable

THE SMALL BUSINESS FINANCE BIBLE

Let's take Abigail's Catering Service as a hands-on example of setting up a digital bookkeeping system:

Abigail decided it was time to move from her old-fashioned ledger to an online accounting platform. She followed these practical steps:

1. She researched and selected a cloud-based bookkeeping software tailored for small businesses that came recommended for simplicity and comprehensive features.
2. Abigail set up her account by entering basic business information such as her company name, financial year start date, tax information, etc.
3. She connected her business bank account and credit card to the software which allowed all her transactions to be automatically imported into the platform each day.
4. For each transaction that appeared in her account, Abigail checked the categorization suggested by the software – such as 'Supplies', 'Equipment', 'Salaries' – making adjustments where necessary for accuracy.
5. Every month, Abigail used the reporting tool provided by her software to track her profit margins, identifying which areas of her business were most lucrative.

Whether you choose traditional or digital methods depends on various factors including your budget, the size of your business, personal preference on technology use, and the complexity of your transactions. Most importantly, no matter which method you use it's imperative that regular maintenance is carried out – such as reconciliations – ensuring that records are accurate; inaccurate bookkeeping can lead to serious legal consequences and can affect business decisions. Remember that transitioning from one system to another can be difficult; so thoroughly research both options before deciding which path is right for your small business finance management needs.

ESSENTIAL BOOKKEEPING TASKS FOR DAILY OPERATIONS

A system of daily bookkeeping tasks ensures that you maintain accurate records and stay on top of your business's financial movements. Here are some fundamental bookkeeping tasks you should incorporate into your daily routine to help streamline your small business finance management.

THE SMALL BUSINESS FINANCE BIBLE

1. Record Financial Transactions: Every single day, money flows in and out of your business. It's crucial to record all these transactions with precise details such as date, amount, and purpose. Use accounting software or a simple spreadsheet to capture sales, purchases, receipts, and payments.

2. Review Cash Position: At the start of each day, review your cash on hand, which includes bank balances and petty cash reserves. This will inform you about how much cash is available for daily operations and if you need to make any immediate cash flow decisions.

3. Monitor Outstanding Invoices: Keep track of invoices that have been issued but not yet paid. Follow up with customers who have overdue bills to ensure timely payments and maintain healthy cash flow.

4. Verify Vendor Bills and Schedule Payments: Record incoming bills from vendors, suppliers, or service providers. Verify the amounts and due dates, then schedule payments to avoid late fees or service interruptions.

5. Reconcile Transactions with Bank Records: As transactions occur throughout the day, it's imperative to match them against your bank records—this process is known as reconciliation. Catch discrepancies before they turn into bigger problems down the line.

6. Manage Petty Cash: If your business uses petty cash for small office expenses or sundries, document all withdrawals and replenishments regularly to maintain a clear record of these transactions.

7. Organize Receipts and Financial Documents: Gather and categorize receipts, ensuring all expenses are accounted for properly. Store them either physically in an organized manner or digitally using document scanners or mobile apps.

8. Prepare For The Next Day: At the end of each business day, set yourself up for success by preparing a list of financial tasks for the next day—such as deposits to make or calls regarding accounts receivables.

THE SMALL BUSINESS FINANCE BIBLE

In addition to these tasks, keep your bookkeeping efficient with a regular schedule:

TASK	FREQUENCY
Record Transactions	Daily
Review Cash Position	Daily
Monitor Outstanding Invoices	Daily
Verify Vendor Bills	As received
Schedule Payments	Prior to Due Date
Reconcile Transactions	Daily/Weekly
Manage Petty Cash	As needed
Organize Receipts	Daily

Adhering to this schedule ensures that nothing falls through the cracks in your daily financial management process. By integrating these essential bookkeeping practices into your daily routine, you will provide yourself with valuable insights into the financial status of your company — facilitating better decision-making capabilities regarding expenditure and investment strategies.

Remember that accurate bookkeeping not only aids in day-to-day decisions but also prepares you for tax season, potential audits, and can be compelling evidence of your company's value in the event of seeking investments or selling your business.

CHAPTER

12

MAINTAINING ACCURATE RECORDS

THE SMALL BUSINESS FINANCE BIBLE

As a small business owner, keeping an accurate record of your financial transactions is indispensable. Not only does it ensure compliance with legal standards, but it also provides critical insight into your business's financial health. Let us outlines some fundamental best practices to adopt in your bookkeeping routine.

1. Be Meticulous with Documentation: Every financial transaction should have a corresponding documentation, such as invoices, receipts, bank statements, or payment notes. Ensure that these documents are well-documented and filed systematically. It's not enough to just record the numbers; having the physical or digital paperwork to back them up is essential.

2. Use Consistent Recording Methods: Whichever method you choose for recording transactions (cash basis or accrual), stick with it throughout the fiscal year. Consistency is key because it allows for more accurate trend analysis and financial reporting. It also prevents confusion when preparing tax returns or auditing your accounts.

3. Reconcile Regularly: Reconciliation is the process of verifying that your records match up with bank statements and other financial documents. This should be done at regular intervals—monthly is recommended—to catch any discrepancies early on. Mistakes can happen, and prompt detection makes them easier to resolve.

4. Implement a Double-Entry System: The double-entry system is a foundational concept in accounting where every entry to an account requires a corresponding and opposite entry to a different account. For instance, when you make a sale, you would record the income but also note the reduction in inventory. This method promotes balance and accuracy in financial statements.

5. Categorize Transactions Appropriately: When recording transactions, use clear and consistent categories like *'utilities'*, *'supplies'*, *'sales'*, etc., so you can track where money comes from and where it's going. Proper categorization assists in analyzing business expenses and earnings more efficiently.

6. Use Bookkeeping Software: There are many affordable (and even free) bookkeeping software options tailored to small businesses that automate much of the transaction recording process. They can reduce human error and save time by connecting directly to your bank account and categorizing transactions for you.

THE SMALL BUSINESS FINANCE BIBLE

7. Stay Up-to-date with Regulations: Tax laws and financial regulations change regularly, which can affect how you need to record certain transactions. Make sure to stay informed about these changes or work with a professional accountant who can provide timely updates.

8. Train Your Staff: If anyone else in your organization is responsible for handling money or recording transactions, ensure they are adequately trained on how important accurate financial reporting is as well as on the systems you have in place.

9. Secure Your Records: Both paper-based records and digital bookkeeping systems need to have strong security measures in place to prevent unauthorized access or data breaches that could compromise the integrity of your financial data.

10. Review Cash Flow Often: Keep an eye on cash flow—the amount of cash being transferred into and out of the business. Understanding cash flow patterns can help anticipate future needs or identify potential shortages before they become problems.

MONTHLY RECONCILIATION CHECKLIST		
TASK	DESCRIPTION	COMPLETED (YES/NO)
Match Receipts	Verify that receipts match recorded transactions	
Bank Statement Reconciliation	Ensure bank statement amounts align with internal records	
Credit Card Reconciliation	Check credit card statements against receipts and records	
Petty Cash Reconciliation	Count petty cash and match against ledger entries	
Review Payroll	Verify payroll expenses align with employee hours/timesheets	
Inventory Check	Cross-check inventory records with actual stock levels	

THE SMALL BUSINESS FINANCE BIBLE

This checklist provides a practical framework to ensure that all vital elements of your business's finances are reviewed regularly for discrepancies. By incorporating these best practices into your business's routine, you will create a robust system for managing financials—one that not only serves present requirements but also scales as your enterprise grows.

TIPS FOR ORGANIZING RECEIPTS, INVOICES, AND FINANCIAL DOCUMENTS

Maintaining a clear record of financial transactions is not simply a matter of staying organized; it's also about legal compliance, accurate financial reporting, and ensuring you can maximize tax deductions. Keeping receipts, invoices, and other financial documents well-organized aids in the smooth management of cash flow and budgeting. It helps track expenses accurately, thereby giving a true picture of the business' health. Moreover, organized records can save considerable time and stress during the annual tax filing season, when every minute spent rifling through papers is one not spent on growing your enterprise.

Let's tackle **receipts** first. Receipts are proof of your business transactions and vital come tax time or whenever you need to track business spending. To keep them organized, create a system that works for you; this might be a physical filing cabinet or a digital storage solution. If you go digital, numerous apps can scan and categorize receipts for you. Whichever method you choose, make it a habit to record receipts immediately after purchase. To avoid losing them, consider dedicating a specific place in your work area where all receipts go before processing.

For *physical receipts*, label envelopes or folders by month or type of expense – whichever suits your business better. At the end of each day or week, depending on the volume of transactions, file away the receipts in the designated spots. For instance, *'Gas - March'* or *'Office Supplies - March'*. Always write on the receipt what it was for if it's not immediately clear. If you've chosen digital storage, make sure to back up your data regularly to prevent loss due to technical failures.

Invoices are next on our list. These are equally crucial because they relate directly to your income – they represent the sales you've made. All invoices should be stored safely whether digital or hard copy. A consistent and persistent system will make invoice tracking straightforward – which is important when chasing up late payments or forecasting revenue.

If using a *paper system*, assign each invoice a number if they don't already have one from a sequenced invoice book and file them numerically or by client in binders or file folders labeled clearly with dates and content details such as *'Client X invoices - Q1'*. This helps in quickly locating any invoice when needed. For those adopting technology solutions like cloud-based accounting software; they can be lifesavers. These systems store invoices electronically and often include features that allow you to send reminders for payments automatically.

Now onto broader **financial documents** – think bank statements, tax filings, salary records - these documents form the backbone of your business's financial history. Organizing them might seem daunting but keeping them properly sorted will save you countless hours in the long run. Start by separating each type of document into its own distinct group. Each group should have an easily identifiable home; whether that's a drawer in a filing cabinet labeled 'Bank Statements 202X' or a digital folder named *'Tax Documents 202X'*. Within their respective homes compile the documents chronologically. This simplifies the process when searching for specific items later on.

Additionally, designate regular times for updating this system – perhaps when you do your books monthly or at least quarterly; so that the task doesn't become overwhelming at year-end. Remember, retention is key. The IRS can audit your business's finances going back several years so having everything accessible is critical. Consult with an accountant regarding how many years' worth of various documents must be stored.

By following these simple steps – immediate sorting and recording of receipts into clearly marked spaces; sequential filing and prompt processing of invoices; and chronological categorization of broader financial statements – you will simplify what can be one heck of an organizational headache.

Keep it consistent; check and update regularly; back up frequently (especially if going digital) and lean into tech solutions if they serve your operational style because staying organized doesn't just mean keeping a tidy workspace—it means ensuring the financial heartbeat of your small business is strong and steady.

THE SMALL BUSINESS FINANCE BIBLE

ARCHIVAL STRATEGIES FOR LONG-TERM RECORD RETENTION

Archival strategies are essential in ensuring that vital records of a business are preserved for the long haul. Such strategies help in safeguarding historical data which can be referred to for future trends, legal requirements, and historical records. Moreover, effective long-term record retention is crucial for maintaining the integrity and continuity of a company's history and operations. Imagine needing access to a critical financial document from ten years ago, only to find it has been lost due to poor archiving methods. This scenario highlights the importance of good archival practices.

For small businesses in particular, establishing solid archival strategies can be seen as setting the foundation for enduring success. As companies evolve, the ability to reflect on past decisions through documented records can provide invaluable lessons for future strategy formation and refinement. Properly archived documents also facilitate compliance with industry regulations and legal standards, which may require businesses to maintain records for a specified number of years.

In developing an archival strategy that ensures long-term record retention, small businesses should first identify what documents need to be kept. Often, this includes financial statements, tax returns, transaction histories, contracts, company minutes, and other documents that have legal or operational significance. Once identified, these documents must be categorized based on their retention needs; some may require permanent storage, while others could have a specific shelf-life according to business guidelines or legal stipulations.

The use of technology plays an integral role in modern archival strategies. Digital archiving—or electronic document management systems—has become increasingly popular due to their capacity to store large amounts of data in relatively small digital spaces. Small businesses should consider investing in reliable digital storage that offers both robust security features and ease of access when needed. Cloud-based solutions are particularly beneficial because they offer off-site storage that is both scalable as per the business needs and resilient against physical damage like fires or floods.

Nevertheless, it's important not to rely solely on digital methods. Maintaining physical copies of extremely important documents in a secure location is recommended as well—this is known as a hybrid approach to document archiving. Security measures should not just protect against theft or unauthorized access but also environmental factors such as moisture or pests that could degrade paper over time.

THE SMALL BUSINESS FINANCE BIBLE

To organize documents for long-term retention effectively, consistent labeling and indexing practices must be adopted. All files should be clearly marked with details pertaining to content type and the date range covered by the documents within them. It helps if electronic files follow a standardized naming convention that includes relevant identifiers such as date or subject matter.

Additionally, creating a documented retention schedule helps maintain organizational discipline around which records are maintained and for how long before they are destroyed (if permissible). This policy helps mitigate unnecessary hoarding of documents that take up valuable space without serving any practical purpose. Ensuring staff are educated about the significance of document archiving is another key component of successful archival strategies. Training programs might cover topics such as properly handling sensitive information during document storage or destruction processes.

The role of professional archival services should not be overlooked by small businesses seeking expertise in this area. They offer specialized knowledge about best practices for document management and can sometimes provide secure physical or digital archiving facilities to clients looking for outsourced solutions.

Amidst all these steps towards achieving efficient archives for long-term record retention, undergoing regular audits of archived documents could serve as both quality control and an opportunity for continuous process improvement within this domain.

CHAPTER 13

PAYROLL, BENEFITS, AND INDEPENDENT CONTRACTORS

THE SMALL BUSINESS FINANCE BIBLE

HANDLING PAYROLL TAXES AND REPORTING

Payroll taxes are a crucial part of running your business. It's not the most exciting subject, but understanding this process is essential. Here, we'll break down the steps you need to take to handle payroll taxes and correctly report them to avoid any fines or penalties.

Know which taxes you're responsible for. There are mainly three types of payroll taxes: federal income tax, Social Security and Medicare, often referred to collectively as FICA, and Federal Unemployment Tax (FUTA). State and local taxes can also apply depending on where your business is located.

Every employee must complete a Form W-4 when they start working for you. This form will tell you how much federal income tax you should withhold from their paycheck. As for FICA, the current rates are 6.2% for Social Security and 1.45% for Medicare on both employee and employer up to certain wage limits.

The Federal Unemployment Tax is paid by employers only and is not deducted from employees' wages. The FUTA rate is 6% on the first $7,000 you pay each employee as wages during the year. However, you may be able to receive a credit of up to 5.4% if you pay state unemployment taxes timely. This could lower your federal rate to as little as 0.6%.

Now let's talk about how often these taxes need to be deposited with the IRS. The schedule can be monthly or semi-weekly depending on the total tax liability your business has reported during a lookback period established by the IRS. You must also report payroll taxes regularly using specific forms such as Form 941 for federal tax returns on a quarterly basis or Form 940 annually for FUTA taxes.

THE SMALL BUSINESS FINANCE BIBLE

To simplify understanding of these concepts, please refer to the table below:

PAYROLL TAX TYPE	RESPONSIBLE PARTY	RATE	FORM	DEPOSIT FREQUENCY
Federal Income	Employee & Employer	Depends on employee's W-4	Form 941	Monthly/Semi-weekly
Social Security	Employee & Employer	6.2% (each)	Form 941	Monthly/Semi-weekly
Medicare	Employee & Employer	1.45% (each)	Form 941	Monthly/Semi-weekly
Federal Unemployment (FUTA)	Employer Only	6%, may credit up to 5.4%	Form 940	Annually

Keep in mind that reporting and deposit schedules are not suggestions; they are requirements with deadlines that have to be met.

So, what happens after withholding these taxes from employees' paychecks? You must then deposit these withholdings along with your share (for FICA) to an authorized bank or financial institution using electronic funds transfer, specifically through the Electronic Federal Tax Payment System (EFTPS).

Documentation is vital in all business operations but particularly so in payroll taxes whereby every figure needs evidence backing it up whether it's deductions or contributions made by both employees and employers. Maintaining meticulous records not only helps when it's time to report and pay your payroll taxes but also in case you are ever audited by IRS. Keeping payroll - related documentation such as time sheets, wage calculation methods, tax deposits schedules can protect your business from potential problems down the line.

Avoiding common mistakes can save you headaches later on; this includes always verifying employee information, keeping up-to-date with changes in tax law, using accurate calculations for withholding and ensuring timely deposits of all withheld payroll taxes. Above all, remember that staying organized with your records and staying informed about current tax laws goes a long way in managing payroll taxes effectively.

MANAGING EMPLOYEE BENEFITS

Employee benefits are an integral part of any small business's strategy, serving not only as a mechanism for attracting and retaining top talent but also as a tool for enhancing employee satisfaction and productivity. The thoughtful management of these benefits can make your business stand out among competitors.

Typically, beyond the standard salary, benefits might include health insurance, dental insurance, vision care, retirement saving plans, paid time off (PTO), sick leave, and perhaps even perks like gym memberships or educational assistance programs. Effective management requires a strategic approach:

STEP 1. ASSESS YOUR BUSINESS NEEDS:

Evaluate your business size, financial capacity, industry standards, and employee demographics. Understanding these aspects will help you pinpoint which benefits are most relevant to your staff and what you can afford.

STEP 2. SURVEY EMPLOYEES:

Conduct surveys or hold focus group discussions to determine their needs and preferences regarding benefits. This inclusive approach not only enhances employee morale but also ensures the relevancy of the benefits you plan to offer.

STEP 3. RESEARCH OPTIONS:

Research various benefit packages and providers. Balance cost against value; sometimes investing in a slightly more expensive plan can pay off in terms of employee health and productivity.

STEP 4. SELECT BENEFITS:

With research in hand and knowing what your employees value, select a range of benefits that align with their needs and your business goals. Remember diversification; offering a variety of options gives employees the opportunity to choose benefits that best fit their individual situations.

STEP 5. COMMUNICATE CLEARLY:

Once you've selected the benefits package, it's key to communicate clearly with your employees about what is available to them and how they can participate. Provide simple explanations and instructions on enrollment processes. Be transparent about any costs they may need to cover.

STEP 6. ADMINISTER PLANS:

For smooth administration of benefits, consider using a Human Resources Information System (HRIS) that manages enrollment periods, maintains records of elected benefits, and tracks usage. An HRIS can streamline operations and reduce manual errors.

STEP 7. REVIEW REGULARLY:

The job market is dynamic; regularly reviewing your benefits package ensures it stays competitive and relevant. Keep abreast of changes in legislation that might affect health insurance or retirement plans. Additionally, as your business grows and evolves so might the needs of your employees; adapt your offerings accordingly.

Managing employee benefits doesn't have to be overwhelming if approached methodically. By taking time to understand both the needs of your business and those of your employees, you set the stage for creating a work environment that is supportive and rewarding — an asset in today's

THE SMALL BUSINESS FINANCE BIBLE

competitive job market. Craft a robust strategy around these steps and see how well-managed employee benefits can lead to a more stable, satisfied workforce which bodes well for the success of your business.

WORKING WITH INDEPENDENT CONTRACTORS

Hiring independent contractors can be the perfect solution for many small business finance dilemmas. The flexibility it offers is unparalleled. Contractors can be brought in to manage specific projects or during peak periods without the long-term commitments associated with hiring full-time employees. This means payroll flexibility—a must for businesses whose cash flow might ebb and flow unpredictably. The expertise independent contractors can bring to the table is invaluable. They often have specialized skills that are cost-prohibitive to develop in-house or irrelevant to the core team's functions.

Furthermore, working with independent contractors sidesteps a lot of bureaucratic overhead. For instance, businesses are freed from withholding income taxes, paying employer Social Security and Medicare taxes, and complying with many of the requirements enforced on employers like unemployment compensation contributions. However, navigating this terrain requires a fine balance between reaping these benefits and managing legal aspects and labor relationships effectively.

When considering working with an independent contractor, it's crucial to understand what differentiates them from an employee. The Internal Revenue Service (IRS) applies certain criteria to classify workers as independent contractors or employees. It mainly boils down to control and independence in financial and behavioral aspects—how much control the business has over what the worker does and how they do their job, and how the business aspects of the worker's job are managed.

The next step is ensuring all agreements with your contractor are in writing. This protects both parties legally and sets clear expectations about work parameters, deadlines, rates of pay, who provides tools or materials if necessary, confidentiality matters, and how disputes will be resolved. A written contract not only reduces risk but acts as a point of reference for both parties throughout their working relationship.

An underestimated aspect of managing independent contractors is maintaining proper records. Not only do you need to keep detailed financial records for tax purposes — like payments made

THE SMALL BUSINESS FINANCE BIBLE

throughout the fiscal year — but also track milestones and project specifics. This helps manage performance while protecting your business against any misclassification issues that may arise.

In terms of compensation, decide whether you'll pay by the hour, by deliverable, or a mix depending on tasks complexity or importance; what's vital here is to align payment schedules with your cash flow cycles as tightly as possible so that paying your contractors doesn't strain your finances.

While it's tempting to work with good contractors repeatedly because of their familiarity with your business processes, it's also important not to blur lines that might lead government entities to view them as employees. The key here is establishing boundaries where contractors retain control over their work hours, methods, and decision-making about how they complete tasks.

A practice often overlooked when hiring an independent contractor is considering their cultural fit within your company. Yes, even someone who isn't an employee needs to understand and respect the way your company operates internally and externally with clients or customers.

Communicating transparently about expectations and feedback is crucial throughout your engagement with a contractor. Regular check-ins may not seem necessary since they operate independently—yet aligning regularly ensures both sides are satisfied with how projects progress.

Unfortunately, sometimes things don't go as planned. You may need an exit strategy for ending contractual relationships that aren't working out as expected. Develop fair processes for termination of contracts in advance, including notice periods and termination fees if applicable.

Building a network of reliable contractors who deliver quality work can be incredibly beneficial for a small business on a lean budget needing specialized skills temporarily or seasonally. Regularly assess whether their roles could become permanent positions or if staying flexible continues to serve your business better financially.

It's essential not only to stay abreast of best practices but also regulatory changes concerning independent contractors; falling behind on these updates could land your business in hot water financially and legally. Working successfully with independent contractors isn't without its challenges but mastering this skill set can propel your small business financially while keeping you agile in a market that increasingly values adaptability over traditional static structures.

CHAPTER 14

PERIODIC REVIEWS & RECONCILIATIONS

THE SMALL BUSINESS FINANCE BIBLE

PERFORMING MONTHLY BOOKKEEPING CHECKUPS

Maintaining accurate financial records is the cornerstone of any successful business, and performing monthly bookkeeping checkups can be one of the most effective practices a small business adopts. Regular checkups ensure that your financial information is up-to-date, which is crucial for making informed business decisions. As a small business owner, it allows you to catch errors early, stay compliant with tax laws, and manage your cash flow better. Moreover, it provides a steady pulse on your business's financial health, allowing you to track progress toward your financial goals and adjust strategies as needed.

By staying consistent with monthly checkups, you also prepare your business for smoother year-end reporting. It prevents the last-minute rush to update financial records before filing taxes or presenting documents to investors. In essence, monthly bookkeeping acts as a preventive measure against financial mismanagement and helps in building a strong foundation for long-term business stability.

STEP 1. GATHER YOUR FINANCIAL DOCUMENTS:

Collect all relevant financial statements: bank statements, credit card statements, invoices, receipts, payroll records, and any other documentation reflecting the business's transactions for the month. Ensure that all records are complete and organized to facilitate the following steps.

STEP 2. RECONCILE BANK ACCOUNTS:

The process of reconciling involves comparing your own records (your ledger) to the bank statements. Any differences should be investigated and resolved. Discrepancies can occur due to bank fees, transaction timing differences, or errors in your records. Using accounting software can help automate part of this process.

THE SMALL BUSINESS FINANCE BIBLE

STEP 3. REVIEW ACCOUNTS RECEIVABLE:

Analyze the list of customers who owe you money. How old are these debts? Are there any overdue? Actions may be required to collect on those accounts or decide if some need to be written off as bad debt.

STEP 4. INSPECT ACCOUNTS PAYABLE:

Inspect what your business owes to ensure no upcoming payments are missed – this will help maintain good relationships with suppliers and avoid late fees.

STEP 5. ANALYZE PROFIT AND LOSS STATEMENT:

A Profit and Loss (P&L) statement gives you a clear overview of your revenues and expenses over the month. Examine this carefully for any anomalies or unexpected changes in income or spending.

Important Ratios to Calculate:

- 💵 Gross Profit Margin = (Gross Profit / Revenue) x 100
- 💵 Net Profit Margin = (Net Income / Revenue) x 100
- 💵 Current Ratio = Current Assets / Current Liabilities

Understanding these ratios can help assess whether you're making enough profit relative to sales and if current assets adequately cover current liabilities.

STEP 6. EXAMINE CASH FLOW STATEMENT:

Your Cash Flow Statement is an essential tool that shows how well your company manages its cash position. It reveals how much cash is being generated, which funds operations and investments, and if additional cash reserves are improving or depleting.

THE SMALL BUSINESS FINANCE BIBLE

STEP 7. INVENTORY CHECK (IF APPLICABLE):

If your business holds inventory, conduct a physical count to match against your recorded inventory levels. Adjust for any discrepancies noted as they can significantly affect both cost of goods sold (COGS) and profits.

STEP 8. REVIEW PAYROLL EXPENSES:

Payroll often represents one of the most significant expenses for a business. Verify that all payroll transactions have been correctly recorded and reconciled, including withholdings for taxes and benefits.

STEP 9. UPDATE FIXED ASSET REGISTER:

Any purchases or disposals of fixed assets during the month need to be updated in your fixed asset register for tax calculation purposes.

Implementing these steps each month ensures that no aspect of your financial health is overlooked. By staying diligent with monthly bookkeeping checkups, you better prepare your small business for sustainable success and growth while minimizing surprises during tax season or at times when critical financial decisions must be made.

Remember always to store your documents securely after each checkup and update any electronic data backups as part of your closing routine – meticulous record-keeping today forms the bedrock of sound financial decisions tomorrow.

RECONCILING BANK ACCOUNTS

Reconciling bank accounts is a bit like giving your business a financial health check-up. It's the process of making sure that your business's cash records are correct and in agreement with the bank statements. Essentially, it's matching your own accounting records to the bank's records.

THE SMALL BUSINESS FINANCE BIBLE

It ensures that every dollar earned and spent is accounted for. This process highlights any discrepancies between your books and what the bank says. Without this step, you might not notice if there was a mistake in the bank's processing, if you've been overcharged for a service, or worse, if there has been fraudulent activity on your account.

Reconciling accounts keeps your financial reports accurate. When you know exactly how much money you have, you can make informed decisions on spending and investments. It also makes tax preparation easier as all transactions are accounted for and properly documented.

STEP 1. GATHER YOUR DOCUMENTS:
Collect your monthly bank statement and your business ledger or bookkeeping records. These documents contain the transactions you've recorded and those your bank has processed.

STEP 2. MATCH TRANSACTIONS:
Begin with the opening balance on your bank statement. Check each transaction on the statement against your ledger. For every transaction that matches on both records, put a checkmark next to it in your ledger.

STEP 3. NOTE DISCREPANCIES:
Identify any transactions that appear in one record but not the other. These could be outstanding checks that haven't cleared, deposits in transit, errors by the bank, or omissions in your records.

STEP 4. ADJUST YOUR LEDGER:
Once discrepancies are noted, make appropriate adjustments in your ledger. Add any transactions missing from your books but present on the bank statement. Conversely, record any subtracted fees or added interest that the bank has posted which weren't previously on your books.

THE SMALL BUSINESS FINANCE BIBLE

STEP 5. ACCOUNT FOR TIME DIFFERENCES:

Understand that some transactions might not appear on the current bank statement due to timing differences – for instance, a cheque issued at the end of the month might not clear until after the statement date.

STEP 6. CALCULATE ADJUSTED BALANCE:

After accounting for discrepancies and time differences, calculate an adjusted balance from both your ledger and the bank statement. These should now align if all discrepancies have been appropriately addressed.

Now let's take an example with figures to illustrate this process:

DESCRIPTION	LEDGER BALANCE	BANK STATEMENT BALANCE	RECONCILIATION ACTION	ADJUSTED BALANCE
Opening Balance	$20,000	$20,000	N/A	$20,000
Deposit from Client A	+$5,000	+$5,000	N/A	$25,000
Office Supplies Payment	-$500	-$500	N/A	$24,500
Bank Service Charge (not recorded)	$0	-$50	Record Charge	-$50
Client B Check (not cleared)	+$1,500	$0	Note Outstanding Deposit	+$1,500
Ending Balance (Expected)	$26,000	(Actual) $24,450	-	$25,950

By examining this table:

1. We first start by comparing opening balances which here agree perfectly at $20,000.
2. We then move onto adding transactions such as Client A's deposit which again matches in both ledger and bank statement.
3. Expenses such as office supplies payment are also matched.
4. The discrepancy arrives with an unrecorded Bank Service Charge which after being adjusted leads to a new Adjusted Balance.
5. Lastly 'Client B Check' which hasn't cleared yet is identified as an Outstanding Deposit that needs considering within our reconciliation.

After going through each transaction meticulously and recording all necessary adjustments, we've reconciled our accounts accurately reflecting both real cash positions and pending transactions waiting clearance. This tracking ensures our financial integrity remains intact enabling assured decision-making bearing no unpleasant surprises when it comes to managing finances – paramount for small businesses that often operate on tight margins where every dollar counts!

By regularly reconciling - at least once per month - we close any gaps in our record-keeping ensuring continued accuracy which serves as a strong foundation not only for current operational decision-making but also propelling strategic long-term planning forward with confidence.

PREPARING FOR YEAR-END CLOSE-OUTS

As the year draws to close, small business owners everywhere begin the hustle of wrapping up their financial affairs. The year-end close-out is a crucial period for your business as it heralds the finalization of your annual financial records. Think of it as an annual grand cleaning, ensuring that your financial house is in order for the new year. Prepping well for this event ensures a cleaner transition into the impending tax season and provides valuable insights for strategic planning.

The most critical step in preparing for the year-end close-out involves getting your bookkeeping records updated and accurate. This requires reconciling all bank accounts, credit cards, and ensuring all revenue and expenses are accounted for within the correct period.

THE SMALL BUSINESS FINANCE BIBLE

Now, let's journey through imperative actions to methodically shut the books on the current year:

1. Revisit Invoices and Receivables: Evaluate all issued invoices to ensure they've been recorded in the correct period and follow up on any outstanding receivables. Any invoices that aren't likely to be collected should be classified as bad debt and written off to accurately reflect potential income.

A simple table like this can be used:

INVOICE ID	DATE ISSUED	DUE DATE	STATUS	AMOUNT
INV1001	2023/02/15	2023/03/15	Paid	$2,000
INV1002	2023/05/20	2023/06/20	Outstanding	$750
INV1003	2023/09/10	2023/10/10	Partially Paid	$1,200

2. Inventory Assessment: If you possess physical inventory, conduct a comprehensive count to verify records match actual stock levels. Discrepancies can lead to incorrect cost of goods sold calculations and tax liabilities.

3. Asset Management: Evaluate all capital assets purchased throughout the year, including equipment or real estate. Determine whether they're still driving value for your company or if they've become obsolete or fully depreciated – which would entail removing them from your books.

4. Expense Analysis: Scrutinize all recorded expenses thoroughly to ensure they were necessary and appropriately categorized. Remember, certain expenses may qualify for tax write-offs.

5. Debt Review: Compile a list of all debts owed by your business and confirm that interest payments have been properly recorded throughout the year.

6. Prepayments: Adjust entries for prepaid expenses such as insurance or subscriptions that stretch into the next fiscal year; these should be rightly reflected on balance sheets.

THE SMALL BUSINESS FINANCE BIBLE

7. Close Out Profit and Loss Statements: Transfer your net profit or loss for the year from your Income Statement to Retained Earnings on your Balance Sheet. This visual transition signifies that you have indeed closed your books.

8. Year-End Tax Planning: With updated financial statements at hand, it's the perfect time to strategize with a tax professional on possible deductions or deferrals that can reduce tax liability.

Note: Always maintain clear communication with corporate stakeholders during this process to manage expectations accurately.

After rolling through these checks and balances with diligence, you lay down a transparent pathway for external parties like tax professionals, investors, or potential buyers – showcasing confidence in managing your business finances. Here's a basic timetable chart as tangible guidance through close-out:

MONTH	ACTION ITEM
October	Begin Preparing Documents
November	Reconcile All Accounts; Follow Up on Receivables
Early December	Complete Inventory Count
Mid December	Review Assets; Categorize Expenses
Late December	Address Debt; Adjust Prepayments
End of December	Finalize Income Statement; Meet with Tax Advisor

Moving firmly through this checklist can offer revelations about financial health – propelling future planning on solid fiscal footings.

CHAPTER

15

USING BOOKKEEPING DATA TO IMPROVE BUSINESS DECISIONS

THE SMALL BUSINESS FINANCE BIBLE

While it's considered a clerical task, the data gathered through bookkeeping can become a wellspring of strategic insights, enabling savvy business owners to make informed decisions that can steer their ventures toward greater heights. Let's begin with the cornerstone of any bookkeeping system – **categorization**. Each transaction must be correctly categorized to provide valuable information. Categorizing sales revenues apart from service revenues, for example, lets you see which line of products or services is your most significant income generator. If you're running a bakery, you could track how much you make from wedding cakes against daily pastry sales. This insight alone can inform you where to focus your marketing efforts.

Next up - **analyzing expenses**. By breaking down expenses into categories like utilities, raw materials, and employee salaries, you have a trail of bread crumbs leading straight to opportunities for cost saving. Perhaps your utility costs are high. Could better insulation or more efficient equipment reduce those bills? Or maybe there's an unexpected spike in material costs—time to negotiate with suppliers or seek alternatives.

It's not just about tracking static numbers; it's about **understanding patterns and trends** over time. If bookkeeping reveals that customer payments slow down during certain months, this is critical knowledge for cash flow management. To counteract this seasonal dip in cash reserves, you might plan ahead by arranging a timely marketing campaign or negotiating better payment terms with your vendors well in advance.

Debts and liabilities are another chapter within your bookkeeping ledger that demands attention. Are debts being paid off promptly? Is the interest manageable? Regular analysis of debt can help you decide if it's time to restructure debt or even pay it off early to save on interest costs, thus freeing up more capital for investment in growth opportunities.

Inventory management also benefits greatly from detailed bookkeeping data. Knowing exactly what has been sold and what remains on your shelves can eliminate overstocking (which ties up valuable capital) as well as understocking (which can lead to lost sales). This information is crucial for making strategic decisions about product ordering and stock control measures such as just-in-time ordering or bulk discounts.

The heart of strategic insights lies in the ability to predict upcoming challenges and opportunities based on past performance and current trends. For example, if your service business notices an uptick

THE SMALL BUSINESS FINANCE BIBLE

in one-time clients versus repeat clients through record analysis, perhaps it's time to implement loyalty programs to keep customers coming back.

Financial ratios gleaned from bookkeeping are also tools of enlightenment for small businesses. The quick ratio, debt-to-equity ratio, and profit margin all tell stories of their own—stories about liquidity, financial health, and operational efficiency respectively. Each ratio provides a snapshot that, when taken together over time, creates a moving picture showing where your business has been and where it might be going.

Don't forget the power of *integrating bookkeeping with taxes*—a strategic move that many successful businesses employ to their benefit. By staying ahead on tax documentation requirements and understanding tax deductions thoroughly, you can use bookkeeping data not only as an archive but also as a tool for tax planning that leads to substantial savings.

Remember, each entry made into the books isn't just a number; it's a pixel in a much larger picture depicting the financial narrative of your company. By being attentive to what the numbers are saying each day through simple yet diligent analysis practices, small businesses can transform routine record-keeping into a foundational strength driving growth and sustainable progress.

COST-BENEFIT ANALYSIS FOR BUSINESS INVESTMENTS

Investing in your business always comes with its share of risks and opportunities. It's like venturing into a dense forest where the right path can lead you to a treasure trove, while the wrong turn could leave you lost among towering uncertainties. Hence, the wise adventurers of the business world equip themselves with a compass known as Cost-Benefit Analysis or CBA.

Imagine you own a small bakery that has gained some popularity in the neighborhood. With an increase in customer demand, you're considering an investment—a new oven that promises faster baking times and lower energy costs. The decision might seem straightforward, but is it really? This is where CBA steps in as your guiding light. Let's break down what it involves by examining this simple yet powerful approach through our bakery example.

1. Identify all the costs associated with purchasing the new oven. It's not just about the price tag; consider installation costs, maintenance, any additional training for staff, and potential downtime during the switch-over.

2. Next up: benefits. The new oven might allow you to bake more goods in less time, thus boosting sales. It could also reduce energy consumption, leading to savings on your utility bills. Maybe it even bakes more evenly, leading to fewer wasted products – those burnt pastries no one wants to buy.

3. It's now time to put numbers to these factors – quite literally translate them into monetary values. How much will that increase in sales add up over a year? What do you expect to save on those energy bills? Quantifying these elements gives you tangible figures to work with.

4. What follows is comparing the costs and benefits over a period relevant to your business goals—this could be one year, five years, or even ten years down the line. The idea is to get a long-term perspective on your investment.

5. For our bakery's oven investment, calculate how much extra profit you'll gain each year after accounting for the costs mentioned earlier. If over five years, the additional profit surpasses the initial outlay and operating costs of the new oven, then this venture shines green for 'go'.

6. Bear in mind inflation and the time value of money—a concept suggesting that money available today is worth more than the same amount in the future due to its potential earning capacity. Oppositely stated, consider how much your initial cost will be worth years from now.

7. Also factor in qualitative benefits which can be somewhat less tangible but are no less significant—like customer satisfaction increased due to reduced wait times or improved product quality thanks to your top-of-the-line oven.

8. But what about risks? Of course! Every investment carries its own set of risks which should be stepped through carefully. What if a newer technology makes your new oven obsolete in two years? Or what if market trends change and suddenly everyone is into raw foods?

Assemble all this data comprehensively yet concisely without getting lost in complex financial formulas or statistical jargon. Be honest with yourself - if numbers don't reach expected thresholds for profit or present menacing risks - it may be wiser to hold off on that purchase until more favorable conditions arise or different equipment becomes available. Remember that while CBA helps make well-informed decisions, it's not foolproof. It relies heavily on accurate predictions of future costs and benefits which by their nature aren't 100% guaranteed.

Purchase decisions now become less like guessing games at a carnival and more like strategic choices backed by structured analysis—your keys to unlocking potential growth opportunities for your small business while mitigating risk.

THE SMALL BUSINESS FINANCE BIBLE

Embracing Cost-Benefit Analysis before making investment decisions allows you as a business owner to not just survive but thrive amidst economic ebbs and flows. Cultivate it as part of your financial toolkit and watch as it helps pave pathways through complex forests of business opportunities towards success.

ADAPTING BOOKKEEPING PRACTICES AS YOUR BUSINESS GROWS

As your fledgling business begins to spread its wings, it may become evident that the bookkeeping system which served you well in the early days is struggling to keep up with your company's growth. Upgrading your bookkeeping practices can protect your finances and prepare you for further expansion.

Consider transitioning from a manual to an automated accounting system. Initially, it's common to manage finance using spreadsheets or basic software. However, as transactions increase, this approach can eat into valuable time and is susceptible to errors. A cloud-based accounting platform can streamline processes like invoicing, payroll, expense tracking, and financial reporting with real-time updates and backups.

Evaluating your accounting software features is crucial. As you grow, you might need additional features such as multi-currency support, advanced inventory management, time tracking or integration with other systems like CRM or e-commerce platforms. It is essential to analyze your current requirements and anticipate future needs when choosing the software that can scale with your business.

As you expand geographically or across product lines, it may become necessary to keep more detailed revenue and expense records. Implementing departmental accounting can allocate expenses accurately and reveal profitable and unprofitable areas of the business. This involves dividing your books into separate accounts for different departments or product lines.

Hiring a professional bookkeeper or accountant becomes more vital as business complexity increases. While do-it-yourself bookkeeping might have been manageable in the initial stages of your business, professional assistance can save you money in the long run by avoiding costly mistakes and helping you make informed financial decisions.

THE SMALL BUSINESS FINANCE BIBLE

Regular financial review meetings should become a fixture in your calendar. As businesses grow, owners must stay on top of financial performance more than ever before. Scheduled weekly or monthly meetings with your accountant or finance team help ensure everyone understands the company's financial health and is aligned on budgeting and forecasting.

Adapting your bookkeeping might also mean taking compliance more seriously. Growing businesses often face new tax obligations, reporting requirements, and regulations that must be meticulously adhered to avoid penalties. Regularly consulting with a tax professional can help navigate these new waters.

Let's not forget about cash flow management – it remains crucial regardless of business size. As operations expand, cash flow becomes more challenging to monitor but no less important. Good bookkeeping practices enable precise cash flow forecasting so that you're rarely caught off balance by unexpected expenses or dips in revenue.

Lastly, safeguarding against fraud becomes even more significant in a growing enterprise where owners may have less visibility into each transaction. A sound system of internal controls – including separation of duties among employees and regular audits – reduces risks significantly.

COMPARISON BETWEEN BASIC AND ADVANCED BOOKKEEPING NEEDS		
GROWTH STAGE	BASIC NEEDS	ADVANCED NEEDS
STARTUP	Simple expense tracking Basic income recording	
EARLY GROWTH	Invoicing systems	Multi-user access Payroll services
EXPANSION		Departmental accounting Cash flow forecasting tool
MATURE BUSINESS		Rich inventory & project management Advanced data security measures

THE SMALL BUSINESS FINANCE BIBLE

Adapting bookkeeping practices isn't just about upgrading equipment or software; it's also about adopting a mindset open to change and learning continually about financial management best practices. By being proactive about bookkeeping adaptation, you situate your growing company on solid ground for whatever new challenges and opportunities lie ahead.

Remember, robust bookkeeping isn't merely recording what has already happened; it's about planning for future success by ensuring every dollar is working as hard as possible for your business. This evolves from simple record-keeping into strategic financial management – a cornerstone of every successful growing business.

THE SMALL BUSINESS FINANCE BIBLE

CONCLUSION

The guide tackles the essential elements of small business finance management, beginning with an in-depth look at taxation. Understanding tax regulations and filing requirements sets a solid foundation for any entrepreneur aiming to harness financial success. You've learned about the different types of taxes that may affect your business, from income to self-employment, payroll to sales taxes. More importantly, you've discovered how to minimize your tax liability through maximizing deductions and credits legally, leveraging benefits such as retirement accounts, and employing year-round tax planning.

The legally permissible tax loopholes available to small businesses have been laid bare, alongside guidelines for avoiding penalties and navigating the dreaded IRS audits and inspections. From there, we explored setting up an efficient and integrated accounting system—a stronghold for any robust financial operation. Budgeting, forecasting future performance, understanding debt and equity's impact on financial statements stand as pillars of sound business management.

The book also demystifies financial statements allowing you to read and interpret balance sheets, income statements, and cash flow statements confidently. It covers the negative implications poor financial analysis can have on your operations and teaches you advanced accounting techniques such as internal controls to prevent fraud.

In bookkeeping, critical knowledge was imparted about implementing both traditional and digital systems. Understanding the significance of maintaining accurate records cannot be understated nor can the proper management of payroll taxes and employee benefits. To round off this comprehensive guide, it emphasizes periodic reviews and reconciliations as a means for impeccable record keeping. And most importantly, it speaks on using bookkeeping data to make informed decisions that foster not only business sustainability but growth.

This book prepares you to confidently tackle small business finance management. Apply these strategies diligently and watch them work their magic on your bottom line. Embrace digital options for efficiency, stay compliant with tax laws, perform regular financial checkups, analyze investments wisely before committing resources, and always keep sight of your company's growth trajectory.

THE SMALL BUSINESS FINANCE BIBLE

As you implement these strategies, embrace patience and persistence—much like finance itself; success does not happen overnight. Cultivate a relationship with numbers that affirms control over your business's future. Remember that each step taken is a building block in constructing sustainable growth and resiliency.

So, move forward boldly. May the information empower you to navigate tax season smoothly, execute accurate budgeting forecasts, establish robust accounting systems, streamline bookkeeping procedures, steer clear of potential penalties or compliance issues—and ultimately pave the way for the kind of financial success that every small business owner deserves.

THE SMALL BUSINESS FINANCE BIBLE

APPENDICES

APPENDIX A: GLOSSARY OF TERMS

1. **Accounting System:** A method of tracking financial transactions and keeping records in order to manage a business's finances effectively.
2. **Accounts Payable:** The amount of money a business owes to suppliers or creditors for products and services purchased on credit.
3. **Accounts Receivable:** The money due to a business for products or services delivered to customers but not yet paid for.
4. **Audit:** An official inspection of an organization's accounts, typically by an independent body, ensuring that records are accurate and that taxes are paid properly.
5. **Balance Sheet:** A financial statement summarizing a company's assets, liabilities, and equity at a specific point in time.
6. **Bookkeeping:** The recording of all financial transactions undertaken by a company, including sales, purchases, income, and payments.
7. **Budget:** A financial plan that estimates income and expenses over a certain period of time, often used as a guide for financial planning.
8. **Cash Flow:** The net amount of cash being transferred into and out from a business, which affects the company's liquidity.
9. **Credit:** An accounting entry recording an increase in assets or decrease in liabilities. In terms of sales, it is also the ability to buy something now with an agreement to pay later.
10. **Deduction:** Expenses legally allowed to reduce taxable income thus reducing the tax liability.
11. **Depreciation:** An accounting method that represents the diminishing value of an asset over its useful life.
12. **Equity Financing:** Raising capital through the sale of shares in the business, representing ownership interests in the corporation.
13. **Excise Taxes:** Taxes imposed on specific goods or services such as alcohol or tobacco; generally included in the price of the product.

THE SMALL BUSINESS FINANCE BIBLE

14. **Expenses:** Money spent by a business on general costs such as rent, wages, supplies, etc., necessary to operate the business.

15. **Financial Statements:** Formal records of the financial activities and position of a business. Important examples include balance sheets, income statements, and cash flow statements.

16. **Income Statement (Profit and Loss Statement):** A financial statement showing a company's revenue and expenses over a period time, thereby showing net loss or net profit for the period.

17. **Interest:** The cost of borrowing money or the payment made by banks to depositors for keeping money in an account.

18. **IRS (Internal Revenue Service):** The U.S. government agency responsible for tax collection and enforcement of tax laws.

19. **Liabilities:** Debts or obligations owed by a business that have arisen during its operations and need to be settled over time.

20. **Payroll Tax:** Taxes imposed on employers and employees based on wages paid; used to fund social security and Medicare programs in the U.S.A.

21. **Projections (Forecasting):** Estimating future financial outcomes based on past and present data trends; essential for budgeting and planning purposes.

22. **Retirement Accounts (Pension Plans):** Investment plans that allow individuals to allocate part of their income towards retirement savings which typically offer tax benefits.

23. **Revenue:** Income generated from selling goods or services during the regular operations of a business before any costs or expenses are deducted.

24. **Self-Employment Tax:** A tax consisting of Social Security and Medicare taxes mainly for individuals who work for themselves.

25. **Value-Added Tax (VAT):** A consumption tax placed on products whenever value is added at each stage of supply chain from production to point-of-sale.

26. **Write-off: A** deduction from earned revenue that represents uncollected payments due on customer invoices usually because they're deemed uncollectable.

THE SMALL BUSINESS FINANCE BIBLE

APPENDIX B: CHECKLIST FOR TAX SEASON

Tax Document Checklist

Income Statements:

- ❑ Gross receipts from sales or services
- ❑ Sales records for any asset sales
- ❑ Returns and allowances

Expense Documents:

- ❑ Cost of Goods Sold
- ❑ Operating expenses (rent, utilities, maintenance)
- ❑ Payroll records
- ❑ Business travel expenses
- ❑ Business use of your car (mileage log, gas receipts)
- ❑ Advertising costs
- ❑ Professional and legal fees
- ❑ Insurance premiums

Financial Documents:

- ❑ Bank statements and reconciliation reports
- ❑ Credit card statements showing business expenses
- ❑ Loan statements and interest paid

Taxes Paid Throughout the Year:

- ❑ Quarterly estimated tax payment receipts
- ❑ Sales tax collected and paid to state/local governments

Asset Information:

- ❑ Purchase details (cost/date/place/purpose)
- ❑ Depreciation schedules
- ❑ Records of sold assets

THE SMALL BUSINESS FINANCE BIBLE

Investment Documentation:

- ❏ Records relating to property or stock purchases as business investments

Tax Preparation Steps

1. Gather all financial records.
2. Consult with a certified accountant or tax advisor.
3. Review prior year's return for carry-over items.
4. Categorize all expenses appropriately.
5. Tally gross income, returns, and allowances.
6. Reconcile bank accounts with income/expenses reported.
7. Compile documentation for all deductions and credits.
8. Compare current year deductions to previous years for consistency.

Common Deductions

1. Home office deduction if applicable
2. Business insurance premiums
3. Business interest and bank fees
4. Professional service fees (legal, accounting)
5. Education expenses to maintain or improve skills required in your business
6. Travel expenses related directly to your business

Tax Filing Steps

1. Decide whether you will file taxes yourself using software or hire a professional.
2. Confirm the filing deadline for your specific business structure (sole proprietorship, partnership, LLC, etc.)
3. Make sure your accounting records are accurate and up to date.
4. Complete all necessary forms or make sure your tax professional has everything they need.

5. Double-check numbers on every form before submitting.
6. If you owe taxes, plan out how you'll make payments.

Pre-filing Verification Checklist

- ☐ All personal & business information is accurate (name, address, SSN/EIN).
- ☐ All income is accounted for and documented.
- ☐ All receipts are organized for expenses claimed.
- ☐ Review potential red flags that could trigger an audit (excessive entertainment expenses).
- ☐ Make digital copies of all documents submitted.

Post-filing Tasks

1. Record the date you filed your taxes.
2. Make note of any payments made or refunds received.
3. Store a copy of your filed return with other important documents.
4. Set calendar reminders for upcoming quarterly payments if required.
5. Begin planning next year's tax strategy based on current results.

Remember, each business is unique; therefore, additional customized steps may be necessary depending on specific circumstances as advised by a finance professional.

THE SMALL BUSINESS FINANCE BIBLE

TASK	DESCRIPTION	COMPLETE?
Gather financial records	Collect all applicable income statements, expense documents, etc., from throughout the year.	
Consult with a tax advisor	Discussing specific issues related to your business can uncover unique deductions or prevent errors.	
Review prior year's return	Check last year's return to ensure consistency and track carry-over items.	
Categorize expenses	Organize expenses into appropriate categories following IRS guidelines.	
Prepare documents package	Create a complete packet of documents needed for filing.	
File returns	Submit tax forms by the deadline communicating with IRS/state agencies as needed.	

This checklist is designed to alleviate some of the stress associated with managing small business finances during tax season and help ensure compliance with current tax laws while maximizing potential savings where possible.